Published by EliteFoundationAuthorAcademy®, Ft. Lauderdale, FL.

EliteFoundationAuthorAcademy® is a registered trademark.

Printed in the United States of America.

ISBN: 978-1-7320778-0-5

This publication is designed to provide accurate and authoritative information regarding the subject matter covered. It is sold with the understanding that the publisher is not engaged in rendering legal, accounting, clinical or other professional advice. If legal advice or other expert assistance is required, the services of a competent professional should be sought. The opinions expressed by the authors in this book are not endorsed by EliteFoundationAuthorAcademy® and are the sole responsibility of the author rendering the opinion.

Most EliteFoundationAuthorAcademy® titles are available at for bulk purchases for sales promotions, premiums, fundraising, and educational use. Special versions or book excerpts can also be created on direct request for specific needs aligned with Elite.

For more information, please write:

EliteFoundationAuthorAcademy®

2003 West Cypress Creek Road, Ste. 103 Ft. Lauderdale, Florida 33369

Or email ElitePublisher@EliteFundsFreedom.org

Visit us online at:

www.EliteFoundationAuthorAcademy.com

INVINCIBLE

How to Embrace Failure and Achieve
Transformational Success

EliteFoundationAuthorAcademy®
Ft. Lauderdale, Florida

Inspired Stories of Real People with
Unconquerable Will to Thrive and Be Alive

INVINCIBLE

Words are powerful.

They can be used to edify or teardown. Words imprint, leaving their remnants on the recipient. The power of a word depends upon who utters it and its social context.

The word INVINCIBLE has its origin rooted in Old French and Latin - invincibilis, from in - 'not' + vincibilis. Modern day thinkers, purport in Oxford living dictionaries to define the word to mean, "too powerful to be defeated or overcome" and this source provides the example of its use, as, "An invincible warrior."

Invincibility does not mean a lack of hardship. Rather it is a definitive descriptor of the essence of a soul, who has had hardship and yet, not despite it, but because of these hardships has been refined, renewed and restored to... embrace failure to achieve transformational success.

Invincibility demands action, as it posits that once the vessel has undergone this transformation then one becomes a new creation and is set on a course not necessarily of one's own making, but absolute and of divine origin.

No matter your belief system, there are human universal emotions that resonate to elevate collective humanity, these include Gratitude, Faith and above all Love. But, these emotions without action have no meaning.

Invincible was written by successful real people, who share their life experiences transparently, to not only connect with you at an emotional level but, to provide you with real life wisdom, true-and-tried strategies and solutions, so you too can rise and unleash your Warrior within.

Each story may have points of commonality. Themes of life experiences that are shared. But the uniqueness of each of our Elite Author's story of invincibility is found in the essence of how their experience served to shape them then; and the divine being they are now.

Elite Authors' authenticity and vulnerability is only out-matched by their zeal to not only succeed themselves, but to fund freedom for survivors, who are still in the grips of PAIN, and that need to hear their message of Hope.

One of the greatest gifts of success is the ability of reciprocity. We were not created to live in isolation, as one. We are all part of a collective humanity and as such, when one soul is stifled or lost, we as a human race lose out on all that individual was intended to share with us.

Elite Foundation's Scholars, the Elite Authors in this literary work share a vision to affect a better, more compassionate and empathetic tapestry of existence for the world and those that follow them.

The words of Orison Swett Marden (Dr. Marden, author, founder of SUCCESS magazine, in 1897) serve as a reminder to us of our Invincibility:

There is no failure for the person who realizes their power, who never knows when they are beaten; there is no failure for the determined endeavor, the conquerable will. There is no failure for the person who gets up every time they fall, who rebounds like a rubber ball, who persists when everyone else gives up, who pushes on when everyone else turns back. ~ Dr. Orison Swett Marden

CONTENTS

CHAPTER 1

WE ARE ALL ONE

We got to help each other out

By: Viviana Malamud

I am grateful to you, the reader, and I am grateful to Judy for being brave, and for allowing me to re-discover her. For telling me her true story, so that I can share it with you today.

I am sharing this story, because you may be like Judy. I am certain that you will be able to see how troubles do end and that your cave does have a light and your abyss an exit. Sooner than you think, the light will shine on you and the exit, as well as the new beginning, will open-up to you. I cannot tell you when, but guess what, YOU CAN! Like Judy, you will tell your story once, and it will give somebody else a LIGHT to shine!

To you who are silently fearful, Lonely, Ashamed, and Shut down I hope Judy's story shared in this book that has a compilation of many different stories weaved within it, inspires you to become the best person, you can be. We learn something new every day, so I hope that every time you pick up this book you will find something that motivates you for the day, to look at certain events or even life itself in a hopeful and courageous way. Through the eyes of an exceptional human being, who carried pain, sadness, sorrow, as well as love, caring, and happiness and who has much more to give to the world. That day by day you will find the best version of yourself.

PART I - JUDY HURTING

HIDING UNDER THE CARPET

I am talking to you, little one.

Do you even exist?

Yes, I know you are in there.

You were always there.

I may not have let you BE.

I voided you.

I left you out. I shut you down.

I pushed you away.

I had to do it, so I could survive.

I am sorry, I apologize.

Know at times you came to life.

You appeared to be present.

You tried so hard.

But no one listened.

You tried to be noticed in so many ways.

I saw it.

I felt it.

Even your veins you tried to cut.

So much pain you've had.

Today I promise you.

I will try.

To always take good care of you.

To acknowledge you.

To give you what you need.

And to let you BE once again.

You can BEGIN!

You may start all over from scratch,

To build a solid base.

All over again.

You were curious, funny, sensual, creative and sweet since you were a little girl.

How did all those charming qualities become your fault?

Where is it written that being funny is to be punished?

How in this world do you need to pay for being curious?

When does your story begin?

When are you forgiven?

This little one was curious, yes, she was mischievous, funny, sensual and so on. But no personality traits or behavior call for abuse. As a child, you are innocent, and you are also too vulnerable. All your life lessons come from those around you. Hopefully, responsible adults that is.

That night, that night Judy was there. Just there. It did not seem like a week night, it was all so unusually quiet. The Street seemed deserted. There was music very far away, the laughs and the cries you could hardly hear, maybe everyone is sleeping. Maybe you could hear a car engine start, some tires braking, distant baby waking, crying for mama to feed him, and again you could hear nothing, the streets were empty, the streets were naked. Naked like Judy, empty like Judy, being wet with his drops of sweat, his scent was so familiar to Judy, her body shock, shivered ... That night. But that night, was not an unusual night...

What began as just a game, had become a routine where Judy just followed instructions and kept quiet. Never told. After all, she needed some attention, and was getting it all from him. She made herself believe she was a special little girl. She learned to do it, and she learned to do it right. She learned to satisfy others NEVER herself.

How does a noble heart, so delicate so kind, grow into a frothy stranger? So, cold does not even feel. Is it that it once was bewildered? It was hurt. It was broken. Cried. Suffered. And was crumbled in so many pieces so many times. There is just nothing left from this heart. Look at me Call me. Tell me. Feel me. Find me. Enlighten me. When there is nothing left.

The light is turned on and Judy can see once again that she can, she can get up from where she fell. She can take life on from where she left it. She can live again. She is trying, she can feel, she can smile, she can laugh. She has done it before and can do it again. She feels PROUD, because this she shares with us today, will impact others, and make her children proud. To know that their mother had tried and tried and tried and never gave up. Will make her feel dignified and Encourage and Inspire, so much!

Into the night

> My legs are open wide
> I am just a little girl
> Do not say Do not tell
> Secrecy is the key
> I will take care of you
> **Uncle**
> **Judy**: Flat Dull
> On to the day
> You are not enough.
> Your hair is not well combed.
> Your nose is not very nice.
> Fix yourself up.
> **Mother**

Judy: Don't feel good enough.

This is black

This is white.

You can go.

You must stay. Do this Do that

Father

Judy: Confused Bewildered

Judy had lost her ingenuity. Her self-love. Her childhood and her youth. She understood the world upside down. Or never understood it. Nothing made sense to her. Her hopes were shattered. Her self-esteem was destroyed, and trust, she did not have any.

She believed she came from the PERFECT family, only to discover later that she had hidden it all. It was like it was all plugged-up.

She had put on a lid on her life history. It was as if she covered it all with concrete.

And yes, it is so hard to start all over again. Her self-love her trust in it was all gone.

It is true that her heart had been broken more than once. But it is also true that she let her heart be broken. She did it to herself she knows that now.

So, it is she who needs amendment.

And only she can do it herself.

Please love yourself.

I am taking care of you NOW.

It is not too late.

Judy is a charismatic sweet little girl. She lived fearful, lonely, silent, empty, shameful, in pain, hiding it all. She did not feel cared. And the messages were always too confusing for her.

She was born in a very poor country in a very privileged and conservative family. Her father had worked very hard since he was a young boy and he did until his last day in this earth.

Her father was gifted, he was a strong vehement man, he was passionate, and extremist, and they all got used to living under his dictatorship at home. He was the LAW in the house. Judy feared her father very much, yet he was also the one who taught her to be humanitarian. He showed her that what they had, not everyone had, and many would kill for it. In a poor country, you don't need to go too far in distance to see the poor people who don't even have a plate of food. He gave them everything he did not have as a child and much more. Her mother, she lived for him. She was his woman, his lady. She did not work and has always been a very sweet and tender woman. But pitifully, Judy can hardly remember mum taking care of her.

As an adolescent Judy was getting double messages. Sometimes dad was too strict or severe, others too permissive. He would not let her go to the corner store to buy candy alone, or to a friend's house for a sleep over, yet he would send her far away to a different country all by herself. That was confusing, to say the least.

She grew up feeling the difficulties of the families, very sensitive and compassionate towards their problems. She excused her family for their flaws, claiming it must have been difficult for them. Yet she could not see her deep wounds caused through the years of suffering. And the results were even harder. Five children, all professionals, well married, well done. Except for one. You guessed it, except Judy.

Judy's history was marked by three divorces, a long history of bad relationships, with many changes over her life. She moved to 7 different countries, work changes, career changes, and so on and so forth.

Judy was self-destructive, and she also started having relationships when she was very young. This started a continual pattern of abusive relationships with addicts, depressive men, and delinquent men. When she found a good guy, she quickly got bored with him, so she would end the relationship. She was extremely jealous, dependent, and needy. It seemed like the pattern was never going to end for her.

Judy was the type of person who would feel more comfortable living her life by going 200 kilometers per hour passing everyone else. Thinking she was ahead even though her hair was standing up on its end with fear. She did not know how to relax and have fun in life. Until she did.

Judy never needed anything or anyone. She thought she was independent, but she was also proud and angry. She was tired of her days with no messages, no calls, no visitors. She felt all alone, did not know what to do, where to live, what to eat, her life was completely empty.

PART II - AID AND TRANSFORMATION

Judy is brave and courageous. She now lives with her children and she gives the very best of herself every day, and luckily, when her very best is not good enough, she keeps on trying the next day, the next hour and by the minute to be a better parent to them.

At times, she still feels lonely, and it feels like she is about to go back to that pattern of abusive relationships, but she recognizes it, by being consciously aware and she is able to stop it by reminding herself, that she deserves to be happy, she deserves to be loved, that she is GOOD, and she will be just fine.

But none of this could have been done ALL BY HERSELF. There were times, many times, that her angels, as she still calls them, came to her. No one is meant to go through life all alone. As she looks back and she sees all these beautiful angels who held her hand when she most needed it. Those who spent the longest hours listening to her endless stories of love and hurt, who gave good advice, and taught her to listen to herself and STOP. Those who lent their homes when she had nowhere to go, people opened their hearts to her letting her know she was loved. She had special mentors. She will never forget each one of them.

Mentors give us moments of joy, feelings of accomplishment, hand us inspiration and motivation and really vibrate with us!

Like you, we all want to find our mission in life, we want to make a difference in this world. Yet, you must begin with yourself. Loving and giving to oneself first, is necessary to be able to take care of others. It takes us a lifetime to understand this. Place the oxygen mask first on yourself. You must finally learn this. You are simply first. Not selfishly but take care of yourself in order to help others too. Judy's children filled all those gaps that she never imagined and more... It is the hardest job she has ever had, and even though it is not really a job, it is a huge responsibility which sometimes slips through her hands. And yes, she gets frustrated. Children do not respond anything like the way we did. It is a long road. A hard one that needs consistency. Balance. Tolerance. Patience. And a Whole Lot of Love. But mainly Judy has learned to accept them and love them just the way they are. And she accepts herself and loves herself just the way she is. And she intends to continue to do this.

You may want to hang on to being right but being right does not fill the feeling of emptiness inside, it does not serve you to be right if this leaves you empty. Transformation requires change, be open to a new reality, your true self, more than to be right. Mark Twain said, "Forgiveness is the fragrance that the violet sheds on the heel that has crushed it." We don't have to drag those feelings around with us forever weighing us down. Forgiveness stops the resistance to love. You don't have to let anyone hurt you, but you need to accept love. Beginning with yourself. TRUST yourself. If you trust yourself, you don't need to worry about trusting anyone else because you know that you will take care of yourself allowing only what is good for you. You stop looking for answers outside. You just come back to that center, that is your heart, and you will always find PEACE. A little kindness gives you peace. That is where G-d lives, within you. And Judy found it. And you will too.

Judy knew she could choose to feel sorry for herself or she could choose not to. She chooses not to. She wanted transformation and she knows now that you are what you think and so she chooses her thoughts. As she wants transformation in her life, she asks for what she truly wants, she has an intention every day and she lives with purpose.

Tears run through her face when she thinks she could establish her first honest conversation with her mother where she could express her real feelings with no hiding. With tears in her eyes Judy learned that she cannot change her mother nor her past. She can only change herself. She can change her own thoughts, her responses, her actions and her Intention. This has changed her life forever. Then she is given a gift, she suddenly could guide her mother, like how her own children have taught her.

I hope this story can inspire you in some way. We all have a story. Judy's was LOVE. Love confused her, and then she could not trust it. She had been abused in various ways by close relatives. And she did not realize until her late thirties how far these events had traumatized her and affected her entire way of thinking, as well as the choices she subsequently made in her life.

She had a dark side to her past and lived a dark path over and over again. She had been able to come out of it in her twenties, but now, at an older age with kids... well, life has its way of doing things as you ask, as you pray, as you are grateful and forgiven. And she was. She reconnected with special people from her past who also had a more connected view of the world and humanity. Some were her mentors and continue to be, others got inspired by her and their connection still creates a profound energy of learning, reaching out, moments of inspiration, a symbiotic relation, no doubts. She started making peace with her past again. As a more mature woman, she puts her heart into every day. She sees life from a different lens now. She no longer feels that she cannot do it. She visualizes, feels stronger, more secure, able to stand up for herself by being more assertive, more loving towards people and caring for herself. She has a more optimistic view of the future. She got everything on her list done, she confronted her fears through introspection, realizations, knows what she needs to change, to create her space, discard what is not good, keep what is good, and now, looking forward to her next challenge!

Because, she has learned that there is nothing we can not accomplish, and while we are here, we might as well try.

Is it possible that the universe aligns so rightfully well?

I thought of all those things Judy needed to do. And those she wanted to do:

The space, the lot, the people to talk to.

The services to provide, the good to bring to this world.

The importance put on the little things.

The love to share.

Use me as your guide.

Take me by the hand.

Let me be. Stay with me.

Let me free.

Fly with me.

Seat.

Breath.

Take it all in.

Feel your heart.

Be grateful now.

Stand on your own two feet.

Don't ever give up.

Look up.

Look down.

Where you are now.

In this very moment.

It is now.

It does not stay.

It is where you belong today.

But tomorrow it may change.

So really look at you now.

Breath it all in.

Live this.

Take this moment.

Smile.

Dream if you can.

Discover what you want.

Fight if you need to.

Be Real.

Be You.

Say what you must express.

Do what you ought to do.

Someone is Always Watching you.

PART III INVINCIBLE

It is true, we forget to recognize our divine self. We forget that somewhere deep inside of us all, it does exist a Supreme Self, that is our divine self, that is our True Identity and it is at peace. Judy had prayed her entire life. And she felt blessed. Yet, she could not hear the divine voice. Once she did. She was able to experience her personal divinity and with much effort she placed her attention away from the past; she stopped worrying about the future, so that she could instead find a place of presence, mindfulness, and regard for herself and her surroundings gracefully.

From the moment, she was true to herself, it all began to change. She was placing all she had learned, all of her mentors and angels 'advice into practice. This was the real deal. Her process of transformation had continued down the path of forgiveness. Mum trusted her.

She showed her feelings to Judy. And they discovered they had similar monsters and shadows which she had never dealt with nor had she trusted anyone to open up about them. In Judy's heart, this opening may have been an opportunity to accompany mum through her own process. It was in this moment of opening, trust and love that Judy knew God was within her. She felt that divine truth took power over her, she allowed it, for she had finally asked for this moment. She had intentionally prayed for this opening, for truth, for forgiveness, for universal alignment. She worked very hard on her path of transformation. Now she was ready to RECEIVE it.

About Viviana Malamud

WE ARE ALL ONE. WE OUGHT TO HELP EACH OTHER OUT.

Writing woke up a part of her that was asleep. And it helped her elevate her spirit again. It made her step on a milestone through her journey. In this Collective work that is dear to her heart, she has gathered insights from her own personal experience demonstrating the power of attainment in her own life. Viviana tells us about the Universe giving us opportunities to discover valuable lessons and being true to ourselves. She shows us to be grateful by welcoming all situations good and bad since each one is an opportunity to help us learn and grow. And as we allow these, God gives us exactly what we need in order to heal. She tells us how we only need to be aware and notice these situations. After being healthy, we all want to be happy, and of course need to be grateful and optimistic.

Viviana tells us her story of Transformation and Rebirth from being a victim to a high achiever, mother, daughter, business entrepreneur, woman and friend. Telling how she healed her emotional wounds, recover, and regain power to live a joyful live. Calling everyone who has been deceived to step up and live the best life they can. By paying attention, listening to your heart instead of isolating and victimizing yourself.

With the ideal to contribute by her own experience and teaching to take responsibility for our own well-being.

Through her poetry and journals, Viviana gives expression of love from her trauma and healing.

CHAPTER 2

PERMISSION TO FAIL. HOW I WENT FROM CO-DEPENDENT AND SCARED TO HAPPY AND ABUNDANTLY FREE.

By: Claudia Zebersky

You were born with wings,

Why prefer to crawl through life?" — Rumi

This story is for you, courageous woman.

The one who knows you are here to do something big; and deep inside you there's an inner voice that pulsates with a profound purpose, but your head is buried in the sand, and you are too tired to figure out a way out.

This story is for you courageous, woman.

The one who have always followed your heart, but suddenly, you have lost your way.

This story is for you courageous, woman.

The one who set out to create a life like you were "supposed to," but instead, ended up losing yourself in the process of building career, marriage, family and now you find yourself unhappy, confused and scared about the future.

This story is for you courageous, woman.

Even though you did things "right," your life has lost meaning and direction.

This story is for you courageous, woman.

The one who cries herself to sleep, secretly wishing for a better life, but has no idea how to make it happen.

This is my hero's journey; a story about endings and new beginnings, about second chances and what happens when you give yourself permission to fail.

This is the story of how I learned to embrace the unknown and mastered the art of reinvention to create the life of my dreams.

Like the legend of the Phoenix

All ends with new beginnings.

What keeps the planet spinning?

The force from the beginning –

- Get Lucky - Pharrell Williams / Thomas Bangalter

Things are not always what they seem.

It is summer 2012 in sunny South Florida, four months after delivering my second child and having just moved to a new house in the Suburbs in a desirable neighborhood with excellent schools. I had just transitioned from working full time at a Creative Agency to a stay-at-home mother. A dream that I had desired for years had finally come true. I couldn't believe it was here. The opportunity to take a break from the busyness of work and family responsibilities to stay at home with my children. Just like my mother did. The husband runs his own business. There is financial stability, and hints of luxury are starting to show up. From the outside, everything looks perfect. It seems like we've made it, right? But, on the inside, we were living in hell.

The word miserable was used more often than not, to be exact; it came out five out of seven years of marriage. Compassionate communication was not existent. Fighting and bickering became the norm. Looking back at it, even though we were married, I felt alone. I was alone dealing with motherhood and housekeeping as my husband buried himself in the office to provide for the family.

We were unhappy. And, for many years I had come to terms with the fact that this will be my life. The life that was chosen for me and that I was now destined to live.

With no change in sight, year after year, I felt a victim of my circumstances. I felt powerless. I felt insignificant. Like I did not have a voice. I was tuned out. We were buried in a sea of discomfort, struggle, chaos, and fighting; day after day. It had become unbearable. The fighting, lack of communication and resistance was bringing up the worst in me. And my husband had become, not only intolerable to me, but to the people around us.

The irony is that I am a peaceful person, I smile a lot, and my natural state is calm and collected. I am a Libra after all. We adapt quickly to our environment and circumstances, and we get along with everyone.

My upbringing was peaceful, being raised in a harmonious, loving family in my native country of Venezuela. My family was not perfect, but I did not experience chaos and struggle on a daily basis. My father was a renowned and successful dentist in my hometown, very involved with the community, funding projects like a firefighter station and leading Rotary Club chapters. He was always in service to the community. Being the youngest of five children, I was not able to witness his success during his peak years, but I was still able to see the legacy he built. At the time, I did not know his visionary and entrepreneurial blood ran through my veins. I did not believe it to be true, so, therefore, it was dormant most of my life.

My mother was the perfect partner for my father. She brought tenacity and sharp intuition that complimented my father's selfless nature. They worked great as a team and built a beautiful marriage. They have always been an inspiration to me, my siblings, and everyone around us.

So how is it possible that I had built such a dysfunctional marriage?

How did that come to be? It did not make any sense.

Yet, during the first four years after birthing my first child. I was so in denial that I thought it was "normal" to live like this, and so I held space, I pretended. I coped. I dealt with it the best way I could; inside my head. I was not open about it with others for a while. I just did not know better.

It was not until my parents came to stay with us for a few months after selling their house in America that my mother started to notice the dysfunction and the lack of harmony. Having my parent's witness what was going on started opening things up. Through their witnessing I was able to give voice to the feelings and frustrations that I was dealing with, but divorce was still not a consideration. I was in too deep in it, to consider that as a possibility.

The breaking point.

Then comes the spring of 2012, when my second child was born.

When he came, the problems maximized. The responsibilities of two children, home, and dysfunction, became too much to handle, and then, it hit me like a ton of bricks. Oh, my God, I said to myself. I cannot do this. I won't be able to pretend anymore. I cannot continue to live this lie. My children need me happy and functional. I cannot raise my children in this toxic environment of struggle and chaos. I will not be able to forgive myself.

That is the moment I realized; it was a matter of life or death. I could not put it off anymore. If I go down, everyone is coming down with me.

So, we decided to seek help, and I found a therapist that could help shine a light on our situation. Although, deep inside me I knew the damage was already done. Still, I felt we deserved the opinion of a professional.

We went to see her and spent an hour and a half sharing where we were, and at the end of the session, the therapist stood silent, looked at us in the eyes and said, "have you talked about divorce? I could not believe those were her first words, but I was not surprised. We let it go too far, and I took it as a sign that it was time to move on.

The thought of divorce scared me. It took me a full year to integrate the word and come to terms with the fact that I would become a divorcee. What would others say? Am I going to be the only divorced single mom in my social circle? How is this going to affect my life? My career?

There were a lot of questions in my head. But I had also armed myself with a potent tool.

YOGA.

Thanks to a dear friend of mine who turned me into Zen Yoga, I set out to find a yoga routine that I could fit into my schedule. I tried going to studios, but with children, I found it difficult to attend evening classes. And so, I looked for yoga videos and found a great one. Oh, I was so happy. I started carving out time for me. One of the things I noticed during this time of turmoil was that I had lost myself in the process. I had no idea who I was anymore. And I knew that this, yoga could get me started on my path to reconnection with my truth.

So, every night at about 8:00 pm after putting my little one to bed, I would close the door in the family room, play the video, and stretch my body. Oh, how that hour saved me. I did yoga consistently for months. It was the most extended period I had been able to practice regularly. I started noticing changes right away. It supported my flexibility and opened me up to bring me to a state of balance, at least, temporarily.

It was an oasis in the middle of hell. Sometimes there was such a stark contrast, between my inner reality and the current reality of my marriage, from connection and peace to fighting, and back again. I experienced such extremes. I believe dancing with extremes was what activated a dramatic spiritual awakening that completely changed the course of my destiny.

The day I met God

The day was October 20th, 2012. Six months after my second child was born. On that particular day, I woke up feeling unusually depressed and like I was going to have a nervous breakdown. I had never experienced this feeling before. As soon as my husband came home, I gave him my baby, I went into the shower, and I cried as hard as I possibly could. But, it was not a loud cry. It was more of a deep silent soul-tearing call that cracked my heart wide open.

I stepped out of the shower, got dressed, sat in meditation and boom. I felt my heart open and received a significant download for about 3 min. It felt as if the entire wisdom of the Universe was being downloaded into my consciousness. I met God for the first time. I traveled through space into the depth of the Universe, saw my life from a higher perspective and immediately understood my place in it and the karmic contract I had made with my husband.

What came out of that experience was a profound knowing and understanding of God and the Universe. I understood that I AM the Universe. I AM ONE with it and therefore had access to its power. I knew right then; my life would never be the same. And it never has. Even though in my heart, I intuitively understood what was behind the veil, my mind had not caught up with it yet. I needed to integrate the information through reading consciously.

And so, my journey into learning began. The first book I picked up was a book about the brain called "Mind Wide Open" By Steven Johnson, which reconnected me to my other passion psychology. Through psychology, I connected deeper with myself. I went from learning about Positive Psychology to Humanistic Psychology to Transpersonal Psychology and eventually learning about the Human Potential Movement. That is when my deep love for transformation and realizing one's full potential commenced. I became fascinated by it, and I understood my Why.

Learning became my medicine

I turned into a voracious reader. I started to notice that whenever I felt depressed, learning would immediately shift my mood and take me from depressed to engaged, passionate and excited. Knowledge was healing. I spent my days caring for home and children, and at night, I would dive into books, webinars, internet research and anything that I could get my hands into on the topics of spirituality, psychology, human potential, self-actualization, life coaching empowerment, and entrepreneurship. I listened to every single coach out there, took a ton of notes and listened to online courses. I never stopped. I became obsessed with learning.

During that period, I also started writing and journaling my thoughts. Some of the original thoughts that came through seemed so far off. I remember writing one time "You are a Goddess with a big mission to heal the world." Goddess? Heal the world? Me? The thought of that possibility, as I lay in the guest bedroom of my house amid divorce, did not make a lot of sense. But I believed it.

I did know early on that I was meant to empower women. Women who felt trapped and imprisoned in a marriage like me. Through my journaling, the name of my first brand, Divine Temple of Bloom came through. I had considered getting a degree in Psychology but knew that would not be feasible or realistic as a single mom going through a divorce, and so I became a Certified Life Coach instead. And I started writing my business plan.

I was very excited. Yet, coaching others seemed inauthentic. I was amid a divorce, still living with my ex and although I started to see a vision for what could become possible, it was still an idea far away from materializing.

But I never stopped believing that I could. I trusted myself. I trusted the Universe. Shortly after completing the process of divorce and before moving out from my ex-house, I sat in the backyard on the grass, and I made a new agreement with the Universe/God. I said "Universe, I trust you. I surrender. Whatever you send my way I will say YES! I invited God to go on the journey with me.

And so, with that, I moved out and set out to create my dream life. A life that felt more like me. I used money from the marriage settlement and took a year off work to heal. At the time, I had not realized how emotionally beat up I was. My self-esteem was low. I felt as if I was crawling out of my ex-house into safety and peace. I had very little energy left in me. But, I took one step at a time, without stopping or wasting time. I worked with a family therapist, energy healers, coaches, and shamans, anything that could help heal my body, mind, and soul. It took time, but slowly I was able to recover, heal and get stronger.

What we want is on the other side of fear.

Starting again felt very scary at times, but I kept myself busy and began attending events from the local spiritual community that were very uplifting. I pushed myself to go to events alone, even when I did not want to, and started connecting with amazing people right away. I did not feel alone or like I was an outlier as a divorced single mom because nobody from that community knew me pre-divorced. They were all excited to meet me and learn more of me.

During that time, I realized divorced had turned out to be a great thing for me. I went from scared to excited about what was next. I started embracing the opportunity to try new things. It was like a blank canvas where I could paint whatever color of life I wanted, and I loved the fact that no one had any expectations of who I needed to be, do or have.

The power of ownership.

I took life by the horns. I took ownership of my life in a way that I had never done before. It felt empowering, liberating and fun!

I decided to invest in myself. And so, I signed myself up for a transformational training that changed my life and gave me powerful tools to create whatever I wanted deliberately. I took myself on in all ways possible. I grew deeper spiritually. I took on a yoga teacher training at an Ashram just north of where I lived. I started hosting women circles. I studied the Universe and the laws that govern it. I understood that if I wanted to change my reality, the changes would have to happen inside. And that, If I wanted to master my life, I would need to master my mind. I was committed. I learned how the brain works and how I could leverage my non-conscious mind for accelerated learning and manifestation. I practiced meditation and the art of letting go. I understood that to become who I wanted to be, I would have to let go of all the past stories that were holding me back.

I started my own business, Purplewing Studio, a transformational branding studio for purpose-driven entrepreneurs like me. I built an amazing brand. I packaged my knowledge and set out to share it with the world, one client at a time. I took my life on unapologetically.

The result, I've had the best years of my entire life post-divorce. And, I do not know a lot of people who can say that.

And now, almost 5 years since I made the biggest and scariest decision of my life, I can say with confidence that I've done it. I accomplished my goal.

I'm living the life of my dreams. I've built a successful business that I adore empowering entrepreneurs to live their purpose and calling by building powerful brands that align with their highest purpose. I have attracted a fantastic partner, the best I could ask. We recently got engaged in Maui, and we will be getting married at the Ashram where I did my yoga training and that he happened to do the training, as well. We moved into a beautiful home together; we are fully aligned with our vision and desire to recreate a family. Our future looks bright. We get along beautifully, and we are working together supporting the holistic Community in South Florida.

My children are now able to experience peace, joy, love, healing, connection, harmony, alignment and truth. They now have a model for a great parental partnership, just like I did. They can experience a mother who is loving, nurturing, present and connected. The word happiness, bliss, and joy fill my vocabulary only all the time. I can show the world that in life, you must take matters into your own hands and course-correct when you find yourself in the wrong path. It's ok to make mistakes. It happens to all of us. What matters is what you do once you find yourself there. Remember that no matter how deep in the weeds you are or how incomprehensible starting again may seem, you are one choice away from the life you have always wanted.

If I could, so can you.

Believe in yourself sister. Arm yourself with the best tools that are accessible to your right now. It does not take a fortune. The best tools that assisted in my journey were provided for free. Usually came in the way of guided meditations or insights shared by spiritual teachers. Trust your intuition, for it is your biggest ally; know that your soul carries the message that will liberate you, that you are part of a loving Universe that is on your side and ready to support you in manifesting the life you want, if only you ask, commit, and surrender.

I am now in love with every aspect of my life. My inner reality is congruent with my outer reality. Was it easy? No. Was it worth it? Absolutely!

I would take myself on, over and over again because there is no more significant and fulfilling reward than to give yourself *permission to fail.*

About Claudia Zebersky

Claudia Zebersky is a Social Entrepreneur, Brand Strategist and Creative Director of Purplewing Studio, a transformational brand development & boutique design studio for purpose-driven entrepreneurs. Claudia has 15 years' experience in advertising, marketing and consulting. She's worked in financial services as a brand strategist and creative director and for an advertising agency on well-known brands, including Autonation, Nissan, Lennar, Party City, Subway, Papa John's, Friendly's, and Pep Boys.

She's also branded start-ups and established businesses in Retail, Marketing, IT, Professional Services, Legal, Health, and Wellness.

Her passion is to empower emerging leaders and conscious entrepreneurs to step into their brilliance by building powerful personal brands that authentically reflect their essence, personality, align with their highest purpose and captivate their ideal clients. She turns passion, purpose and callings into marketable brands that enable entrepreneurs to discover their unique voice, own their power and realize their full potential. After a spiritual awakening that led to divorce in 2013, Claudia chose to begin again as a single mother of 2 boys, completely transforming her life. She stepped fully into her purpose, leveraged her expertise, started her own business and manifested her twin flame. She now leads webinars and workshops on branding and empowerment and is a published author.

To learn more about her, check out her captivating brand at

www.purplewingstudio.com

CHAPTER 3

THE PHOENIX'S PATH

By: Airica D. Kraehmer

Die. Stop breathing. Stop the heart from beating. Stop holding on. Just let go and let it all end.

There is a spirit, a soul, and a body. While the soul can wager a life worth living, and the body can crumble at the right amount of psi pressure, the spirit holds onto to a gasping breath and a faint heartbeat. Not the body, but the spirit. At this lowest and weakest moment, the soul and body beg for release for freedom. Release from all the memories. Release from all the affliction. Release from life.

I believe in God. I believe in Jesus Christ. I believe there is this encompassing healing love available to humanity. These are not words I tend to say out loud, and in full disclosure I question them more often than someone who has been through everything I have should. So, I am not going to knock on your door, and I currently cannot recall last time I attended church. I just know, I do believe there must be more out there than just us. There must be some alpha and omega in which started this biological cycle, and I try to show through my actions His image because in this topic, I find words useless. All in all, I cannot tell you how to live, but I can tell you how to not, just...choose to die.

Let's be brutally honest. The most likely reason you are reading this is not because you want to know my story. There is so much more to it, right? The brutal truth here is, *you* do want to not live *your story*. Maybe at one point it was all worth the adventure and thrill existence offered but not anymore. There is the potential to temporarily outsourcing this pain through this story, and to some degree I hope that it does relieve the discomfort of a life-ending difficult choice long enough to understand it can be permanently relieved. Everyone has their method of *getting through* trying times, and I am sure many other methods work. Note, I am not one to judge such methods or means as I personally have either tried or at the very least most likely considered them myself. Nonetheless, my way may be controversial or not encouraged by others, therefore I am not going to say my way is good or bad. It is just a *way*. Point blank, here it is. I want you to live *with* the pain of your tragic experiences. No matter if you have had your virtue stolen or if a loved one has been taken prematurely. I want you to not deny the pain. I am careful here in my word choice. I do not wish for you to live in it. I want you to live with it.

Yes, here in lies the world dividing difference.

It is not simply going to go away, or even diminish. Some people may claim over time pain fades, but those people do not truly grasp *this* pain we are holding. This pain is not one defined name or causation, but an intense encompassing concept. For instance, losing your mom or dad does not just get better, and no one can be un-raped or un-abused. So, like you may too, I wake up with it as my bedmate and it tucks me in every night.

Sounds hard and borderline cynical, right? Yes.

Too unbearable to maintain? That is your choice.

Let me get into the part that gives me any sense of creditability to attest this message. You may call me Airica, but if you have no clue how to pronounce such a unique gift, my nicknames are Air, Airy, or Phoenix. Dealer's choice. There are a lot of puns or sayings tagged along with those names now, but the names came first. (Which is my answer to the interpretation of Shakespeare's famous words of *What's in a Name*.) So just like air does, I will rise, and if I get burned to ashes, I will rise again like a phoenix. The point here is, I was given a foundation, and I made it into a skyscraper. This is the starting point of my way, and fortunately you were given one as well. Everyone was given a name, and thus we were given a place to commence. I am a pretty thing. I do not say this seemingly self-serving sentence for vanity reasons. In fact, being a pretty thing almost cost me my life, and it questionably did cost me more. Nonetheless, I am the blonde, 5-foot 9 inches size 2 girl you see walking the runways of fashion shows, in magazines, or on your television set. I am a model, an actress, and many more elements. But for now, I will just focus on the model aspect for it is the one which matters here.

I was living my career dream in New York City. I had signed with agency management agency which promised to help me sign with the greatest names in the modeling world: Elite, Wilhelmina, IMG, Ford, One, etc. Life during this time was not easy, but also it was never better. I was the happiest soul on Earth during this time, and the perfectionist in me was content and at peace for the first time in my life. So, when my potential VS (Victoria Secret) angel wings were clipped in the concrete jungle, the love of my life became my personal undoing and nightmare.

There are many names for human exploitation, and some are even not seen as faux pas in American culture. Most will recognize the slogan, "No is always no." or "She didn't ask for it." Human sexual corruption is a hush hush topic inspiring fear in its conversers, after all, no one wants to think about an organized nondiscriminatory crime with targets of their sons and daughters. The overall issue is we, as a community, are scared and choose not to speak about it because speaking means we will need to address it. And if we address it we may succeed, but we also may fail. Again, in brutal honesty, involuntary enslavement is not just a concern to be left to the authorities of the federal bureau of investigation or other government sanctions, but ending it requires the public to face it as one united front.

With the above paragraphs, the dots have been connected most likely between this violent crime and myself by now. Yet, I sit here writing this chapter to you in a peaceful coffee shop.

How so? Because I am also the element of rarity in my survivorship. Add this title and name to my list of elements from before, but with it I suggest to also add 'Thriver'. Each day, I make the choice of continuing my journey in hopes it will one day reach all my dreams and desires. This could be you too -if you so choose. But again, I am not here to tell you either way.

But your pain mostly comes from a different source, right? So, I cannot possibly understand, correct? So, let us address the elephant in the room, and talk about sources in which lead to the thought of suicide and death as the only choice. (There I finally used the dreadful word.) I have been the student bullied throughout high school by the popular girls and guys. I have been the abused girlfriend of a domestic violent relationship. I have been the child begging for her mother's love while her mother was tied in craving her passing father's love and then that of a new man. I have lost a grandparent. I have been the daughter of violent and destructively fighting and divorcing parents. I have been the girlfriend of a beautiful soul as he died too young in his teenage years. I have been the close friend to several dying friends. I have been the stalked and threatened woman holding keys between my fingers in the parking lot. I have been the individual who loved beyond measure to find her heart ripped out time and time again by both men and women. I have been the one crushed by the feeling of failing the yearning of a dream time and time again. I have, but I am not simply that girl, anymore.

Becoming unyielding is a transformative expedition of one's self. For me, it started when I stepped off that unfinished hometown bridge- in the right direction might I add. Then it started again each time I stepped away from that line. I am assured you understand what I mean, and you may even personally know that line. Stepping away or down is where it starts, but there is so, so much more after. You see, once I decided to continue to live, I needed to figure out how and why I should bother. Everything I wanted in life was robbed from me, and the chances of getting back that point were beyond possibility. Anything I wanted or worked toward disintegrated the moment I was finally able to touch in my hands. If I wanted true love, they would cheat on me. If I wanted career success, it robbed me. If I wanted to be free, I was taken. Time and time again, my ambition would become my enemy. My heart and will would be the friend of my enemy, and thus as the cliché goes, would too be my enemy. From the career standpoint, the most logical choice at the time was to decide on a different profession dream, one in which would not bring me ultimate happiness, but I could be content. For me this was to finish health and human sciences bachelor's degrees and join the medical field.

Let me be clear. It is not by any means wrong to change to a less than favorable dream outcome after choosing to live instead of taking your life. If anything, I am proud of you. To survive is the first step toward progression. This is the step of survival, and survival is vital. It takes a very strong spirit to **survive** after their lowest points in life come to face planting summation. Therefore, be proud too. Go on. Survive until the true moment of your God intended last breath.

I personally want more for your life though. I want you to **thrive**.

Timing has never been to fond of me for this light bulb moment arrived the last month before summer graduation. I was merely surviving. I was living a lie to myself and those around me. I was wearing this false pretty smile required to get through the days, to seem like I was okay in front of my family and friends. After a while, they no longer even looked at me like I was withholding from them. They saw my mask of false joy as my bare face. Thus, I did not share what happened in New York City with anyone. The few times I tried to reach out to a family member, friend, or even counselor my soul bottomed out with their dismissive nature or the fear of judgement of others. My honesty was found in my journals and random writings. Words became my closest friends, and the pen to paper understood when human ear could not fathom or be bothered to even listen. It was from my own friends of pen and paper, I came to the realization of my just surviving through the motions of an untruthful and illusionary life.

In the same month before graduation, I met someone who seemed to be everything I wished I was -an innocent soul of no damage. They held a high-end job and a picture-perfect family and friends. They had true love and support backing them. They held no tragedy of loss, no heartbreak, and no damage. I wanted to bathe in the beauty of such a flawless, untouched life. At first, I thought it was an illusion, but once I found it as truth, I was drawn in like a moth to a flame. I was taught through this person life could be beautiful, and people out there can be good and untouched by the horrors of the world. I admit it. I was jealous, but at the same time, so memorized and happy to see this be a truth in the world. It was not my truth, but it was a truth. That was enough to know because it gave me an idea. An idea I too, could find happiness, success, and true love. An idea so bold in the notion of resilience and perseverance. Yet, it was not enough to see someone else know it as their own. It was like smelling a freshly baked blueberry pie, but never knowing the taste. It was contentment, but I needed to find my own *freshly blueberry baked pie.*

I would have started it right then and there if I could have, but life never goes according to my plans. My memories haunted me like a heavy handbag double stitched to my arm. Like demons they informed me of each time I had fallen and attempted to get back up. After so long trying to get up to walk, I found myself too weak to even crawl. Depression settled into my heart, and it poisoned me from within, dissolving me slowly, like sulfuric acid. My spirit was dying from the inside, and I was not even fully aware of its doing. After all, I was safe and content. I was living off second hand happiness. It came to the harsh reality of living other people's dreams and expectations for my life. I went through the motions of daily requirements of work, food, and sleep, and I lived there for almost a year. And while I do not regret this time for I needed it, I needed to be true to my purpose again. I needed to stop surviving day by day and find this purpose.

I grew into a distant person from my friends and family, and even worse, my soul grew unconnected from my spirit. Feeling lost was an understatement. Multiple events transpired to lead to the point at which I felt the need to end it all again. After so much work of surviving, I was exhausted. I was done. I was lonely in crowded rooms of familiar faces, and I felt betrayed by God himself for everything off the list of that *girl.*

I was His child, right?

I belonged to him as his own creation, right?

I was His masterpiece, right?

So, why had I been burned by what felt like the flames of hellfire and left there? Why did I feel I could never be truly happy?

I will not say, God necessarily spoke to me instead I felt like I was leaving voicemail after voicemail, hoping for a callback. In one of those moments that we, "as good humans", try to pretend we do not have, I found myself in a screaming fury at God on nightly walks to clear my head. I was electrified in the consuming rage of feeling like a pawn in a chessboard of queens.

This time when my voice raised, and tears flooded down, I ranted, "What do you want me to do with my fucking life? I was great once, but now I am nothing! I am done. No more."

In this moment, I was ready. Eager to see Him face-to-face for my answers and conclusions. From wrath to still calmness in just moments, thoughts, in which I do not claim as my own, entered my mind.

Not yet. You do not get to quit yet. Tell it and do something about it. The thoughts demanded.

They made no sense to me. It sounded more like a Rocky speech or inspirational Hallmark card. Lucky for me they resonated. Playing over and over in my mind they recited my muddled instructions. Those words were enough to at least let me halt on any lifespan ending type plans I had at the time.

I had been writing therapeutically of my experiences for months, maybe even a year. It was extensive enough to be a novel, and then I found myself amusingly connecting the dots of the resonating words from weeks past. I was given a gift that was being prepared from childhood for this instant. From my mother's father teaching me the art of typing and writing to the point I wrote these pages of human exploration, fallen dreams, and self-affliction, I was being prepared to tell this story from the start of New York to this coffee house chair.

It was not just a story for me though. In fact, it was ongoing torture to continue writing to the end once the purpose was discovered. My drive had to come from my freshly found purpose. This story, this purpose, was to write for the ones without a voice. The ones without a chance. The ones that lost hope long ago. The ones that keep praying and fighting. The ones who are now free. And the ones that died fighting. Yes, I was a pawn in a chessboard game, but that was because I needed to make the choice on what I wanted to be forged into – a bishop, knight, or queen.

Now, I am rising again. Now, I am chasing my dreams again after a long road of healing. I am moving to a new city for the chance at true happiness of creating a difference in my story. I am becoming a part of a valuing my God given family and chosen family of strong individuals who share my calling and passions. I am becoming inflamed by the creation of beauty in what was supposed to be disaster.

I am *not supposed to be* free.

I am *not supposed to be* alive.

I am *not supposed to be* here.

Yet, I am free, alive, and here. And thus, I am invincible.

But remember you were not reading this to know about me, and I took quite a detour to show you creditability? You were reading this to know something more. You want to know how to save a life- your own life. I am sorry to tell you, but I cannot save your life in this manner. I cannot make you choose to live.

You can die. You can stop breathing. You can stop your heart from beating. You can stop holding on. Just let go and let it all end.

But, if you do not, just...choose to die. If you decide to try to survive, and if you dare to thrive. From the deepest parts of the leftover fragments of my broken heart, I aspire to have this story serve you well. Know it is okay to go at whatever pace you choose in your venture.

I will even leave you with this last piece to the thousand-piece puzzle. With it I hope it can alter your mindset as it did mine.

You can fail anything.

I have the potential to fail at being a model, an actress, a FBI special agent, author, master athlete, accountant, physician, lawyer, mother, etc. Failure is always a possibility. In this short life, if you are going to absolutely be crushed by failure let it be by the one true love purpose that brings life to your soul even at its lowest point. Because when you experience the hiccups and points of uncertainty on this journey with your true love purpose, it will be strong enough to prevail. This is the secret that lies within the holding bridge between survival and thriving, and that is when you too can become...dare I write it, invincible.

About Airica Kraehmer

By her twenty-first birthday, Airica Danielle Kraehmer, also by the nicknames of Air and Phoenix, was an innovative model, actress, healthcare provider, and inspiration to those around her. She has been described as a woman ahead of her years, and someone who refuses to give up despite life's obstacles. When asked how to describe herself she smiles stating, "I am 33% artist, 33% scientist, and 33% businesswoman. But 100% going to bring more good and kindness into this world."

Miss Kraehmer graduated from the University of Tennessee in 2016 with a degree in Human and Health Sciences. She was in the top percent of her class, focusing most heavily on the topics of chemistry, nutrition, and biology. While in college, Airica worked several jobs, sometimes two or three at the same time, to pay her way through- including modeling and acting for fashion print campaigns, runway shows, and television.

The Phoenix was raised in humble roots of a small one-horse type town. Her loving parents worked tremendously to teach Airica to place her value in acquiring knowledge and expressing kindness. Despite life not always being easy financially, Airica expresses true mutual love, resilience, loyalty, and cleansed forgiveness are the world's truest riches.

Airica is an advocator of educating oneself in all ways and supporting others in their dreams. She holds certifications in healthcare, finance, business, and studies anything she believes may help her grow. She is now focused on the mission to help bring awareness and an end to involuntary human enslavement. She finds the silent war against human trafficking a personal one in which needs a united front of individuals from all backgrounds. Her goal is to become an active awareness speaker for the outreach of helping trauma victims and teaching preventive measures to anyone who will lend an ear. She desires to be a haven to survivors of human trafficking and domestic violence, and a mentor to young woman who are searching for hope.

While still in her early twenties, Airica is just beginning her journey. Some may believe her personal battles would be setbacks towards progress, but she will be the first to tell you she is fierier than ever. Now feeling like she has found her voice, she is ready to use it for what she calls her "voiceless kindred spirits". When asked what keeps her continuing what seems to be a never ending uphill battle Airica softly says, "Sisu."

As she continues to write more of her inspiring books, she hopes to give survivors and their families the love and hope in knowing they are not ever alone, but deeply loved.

As I am, as such as I be Air, I must rise.

And when I fall. Trust this. Much as a phoenix does, I will rise again.

Airica D. Kraehmer

CHAPTER 4

PAJAMA PARTY!!

By: Wendy Elliott

Growing up I never went to a pajama party with my girlfriends. However, for many years my mommy and I had our own. Almost every night, we slept on the couches, watched old movies and ate wedges of oranges with salt, breaded shrimp with cocktail sauce and drank coca cola.

That was a great time for me, I was a little girl and thought the Pajama Party was all for me. What a great mommy that didn't make me go to bed at a certain time. What a great mommy that allowed me to eat fun things. I was a lucky little girl. That memory amongst a lot of others will always be special, I will always remember them so fondly. Or will I???

Do you ever think about how it would feel to know you are losing your memory, losing your ability to understand what others are saying to you, forgetting how to get to your favorite clothing store? Or even being able to bathe or dress yourself? When it starts to happen do you really know it's happening? Do you know how others are seeing you or thinking about what's going on with you suddenly?

This is something that I never really thought about regularly but I did see a lot of those I loved becoming more and more confused and unable to perform daily living activities. Although growing up in rural WV it was just explained away by claiming that "Hardened arteries" had taken over. I heard and came to acknowledge that this is what happens when you get older, this is what happens if you live long enough. Well I thought, I don't want to get that old ever. But then again, this can never happen to me or to anyone I am close to, right?

WRONG!!

I have the fortunate, or maybe unfortunate (you will see later) luck that the women in my family live for a long time. My grandmother lived till she was 98, her sister till she was 104 and my mom till she was 93. This fact alone would be great other than the fact that although physically they were all very strong and active, their memory and their minds slowly dwindled away. They slowly went from having that light that shined and sparked at anything and everything around them, full of life and love, to being a shell that was lost. Lost to everything and everyone they loved. Lost way before their physical bodies were taken from us. Loosing someone like that is very unusual. You almost start grieving about losing them even before they are physically gone. They do not even know you exist, you look for that one little hint of remembrance, that one little tap on the face to show that they still know you are with them, that you are their loving daughter... but it eventually stops coming all together. They are gone... but still there.

Every 70 seconds, someone in America develops Alzheimer's. By midcentury it will happen every 33 seconds. Right now, more than 5 million Americans are living with Alzheimer's, and as the baby boomers age that figure will skyrocket and the costs connected with this disease will reach into the tens of trillions of dollars.

The math is merciless: According to a report being released today by the National Alzheimer's Study Group about one in seven of us will get Alzheimer's by age 65. By age 85, you have about a 50 percent chance of having the disease. Think about it.

I did. I know I might well become one of those statistics. Alzheimer's runs in my family; my mom died of the disease as did several of her siblings and so did my grandmother. Like millions of Americans, I know the pain of losing a loved one to Alzheimer's.

I don't want this to be a story of loss, I want this to be a story about a very strong woman that was herself INVINCIBLE. One that was proud, one that was loving and caring with a bit of a sassy side to her. This is about my mommy. This is about how this strong-willed woman raised a woman that has had resilience and that has repeatedly come out on top no matter what because that was what is expected. There will be no time for grief, no time for self-pity or doubt. There is only one way and that is to push on and be successful. So... that is what I have always done, always keeping her in mind.

To back up a bit and to be honest in this story, my mommy was really my grandmother. She and my grandfather raised me on and off for many years to allow my single mom to go back to school, get her life in order and get situated. Although I truly believe she tried at that time it never really happened. Therefore, every time she would take me away, I would cry and cry to go back "home." There for a while I had two mommies'. "Momma Judy" and "Mommy Grandmother." It really didn't seem that odd to me at that time, it was just as it was.

My grandparents eventually had enough and put an ultimatum to "Momma Judy," saying that she either had to take me or leave me and let them adopt me. She fortunately chose the latter. Thus, at the age of 5, I was adopted and never had to leave them again to live with "Momma Judy."

Things were fabulous, I was happy, mommy and daddy were happy and I think "Momma Judy" was happy. Then one morning two years later, I woke up to find my life was changed forever. I woke up to lots of voices in the house, some I could recognize some I could not. My mom's best friend came into my room and said that mommy and daddy had to go to work early so, she was there to help me get to school that day. I was "ok" no big deal. I got dressed and went off to school. Went to my first class and started feeling weird, feeling that a lot of people were talking about me, looking at me strange as if I had something wrong with me. Suddenly, I heard one of the kids in my class ask if I had heard about "Pole" the postmaster dying last night. I was not sure I heard that right, they were talking about my daddy. He and mommy went to work early this morning so that could not be true. He is at work just as he always is. I really don't remember what happened next other than I was at the house, there were people all around telling me it would be ok, that mommy and I will be just fine and th-at I could cry if I wanted to. Cry? Why would I cry, daddy was at work right?????

WRONG

My mom was so strong, she made it through losing the love of her life without one public tear, she hosted people coming to the house, she planned for the funeral, she pushed on and went back to work. All this to be able to push through, to show her strength for me, to make sure that those around her were taken care of... Although late at night sleeping in her and daddy's bed alone I could hear her quietly whimper, stifling her feelings by covering her mouth as she finally released all the grief in the world.

I never mentioned it to her then but did so many years later, and she expressed to me that it felt worse than I could have ever imagined. Like losing your sole but knowing that she had to stay strong for me and for everyone else because that was just what she had to do. She lost the "love of her life" how was she going to do that? All through-out this journey God was in her mind and in her heart, she read and took notes and studied to try and find out why things happened this way. Her life had always been hard and just when she thought it was time for a break this happened.

Mildred Hatfield, my mommy, was the second oldest child in a family of 10 siblings. There were older siblings on both her moms and dads side from previous marriages that sometimes lived in the house but not always. Being one of the older siblings she was often required to take care of the younger ones, clean the house and work at the family owned grocery store. She very rarely got to play or have time to herself. She had aspirations to become a nurse, but that idea was squashed by her father immediately indicating that they were all "whores" and he would not have his daughter be one of those. Giving in again she did what the dutiful daughter does, continue to support the family in whatever their needs were. In high school she met and eventually married "the love of her life" Elderson (Pole) Elliott Jr. They were madly in love and could not wait to move into their own house and start their own family. Just as she got pregnant, Elderson was swept away to war. WWII to be exact! He would spend the next 5-7 years mostly away from her and their eventual 3 kids. He didn't get to see Carol, the youngest until she was almost 2 years old. What a hard time for her. She had three kids, her husband was away protecting their country and she had to manage the business they started to make ends meet.

Finally, the war being over, Pole could come home and be with her and the kids. It was hard, the war had taken a toll on the economy and not many had jobs. They managed to get things together and start their lives again. They had enough money to build a house from scratch (where she lived until she passed away) build other buildings on the property to start a movie theater, built a building that eventually became the Post office in which they were working when Pole passed away and from where she eventually retired. Things were good... Until that horrible day when "Pole" at 49 died instantly from a Heart Attack... Now what...how can she go on? How can she raise a young child and still run the post office, she didn't even have her driver's license? She hadn't needed it. Pole took care of it all... Many times, through-out the years she felt his presence. As did I. I knew he was with us both no matter where we were or what was going on.

Remember those Pajama Parties, I loved when I was little, that I thought was just because I had a great Mommy? I had not realized then and not until much later that the reason we slept on the couches and hung out watching movies and ate our favorite food wasn't for me, it was for my mommy. She needed to heal, she needed to be close to me, the person still with her. She didn't want to go to her bedroom all alone without the love of her life, my daddy. She never shared that with me until much, much later.

Fast forward many years, she continued to support me and whatever I wanted to get into and do. I remember her finally getting her driver's license (she drove many years without one, all the local troopers knew when she came through but never stopped her). She felt that since I was older and getting into more and more activities that required her to drive outside the county where everyone knew her it might benefit her to be legal. She followed me where ever I went, she cheered me on and supported me when it was needed. I never realized it but also never taking time for herself, spending time on creating new relationships or doing anything outside of working and taking care of me and my needs. Everything was good... I was good. But was she?

It was never even an option or a conversation that I would go to college. Since I was little both mommy and daddy put money away in bonds each paycheck for my college tuition. So, there was no doubt I was going to do that. I was finally ready to go, finally ready to spread my wings but I didn't even think of what she was going to do without me here. With me gone what would she do? She never batted an eye, she supported me and agreed to allow me to go off to college even though it was 3 hours away. To me 3 hours was nothing. I would come home every weekend I would be a good daughter and make sure I kept in touch. I did, but not to the level I agreed too. I did come home but maybe more like 1 time a month, I did call each week but due to my heavy schedule (mostly social) I was busy and couldn't get away. She always understood. She was always there when I needed her to be tough....

But.... Suddenly, I called as usual and asked if she was coming up to the ballgame, (I was a twirler and was performing at the football game)? She usually always came up with my boyfriend's parents. She said "no" I have plans with Cap. Cap? Who was Cap? I don't know a Cap. Well come to find out since I had been gone one of her old friends from high school had moved back and was "courting" her. I was angry.... I don't understand how this "Cap" was more important than me. She had never missed anything I had ever done. How could she do this to me?

I realize now how selfish I was. How unrealistic I was in expecting her to always be there for me. Because she always was. She was my solid, my life. Now she was with someone else. At that point, I could not be happy that she had found someone to have as a companion, someone that may love her and take care of her. I knew she deserved it, but I was just not ready, I of course questioned this "Cap's" motives. Where did daddy play into all of this? What would he think? It really didn't matter what I thought at that point she had made up her mind that she needed a companion and went away that very weekend and married "Cap." I had a new "father." Hummm very interesting to say the least.

Now what? Well I continued to live my life as did she. She was with Cap, I learned that he wasn't going to go away so I might as well accept him. If he made her happy then it was ok. But I was not too sure he did. Shortly after she retired, to be with him more, and so they could travel, he disclosed he was sick with what was called "Brown lung" something that those working in lots of sand and dusty areas developed. It was a chronic progressive lung disease and was expected to eventually take his life. In the meantime, he would need constant oxygen and would become bed ridden. As if that weren't enough, she had also started taking over the care of my slightly then dementia laden grandmother. So now when she thought she was going to be able to once again be happy, live life easily, she became a caregiver to both her husband and her mother. Once again never complaining never thinking "why me" she did what she needed to do. Take care of those that needed her attention.

About this time mommy started realizing that she herself was having some physical ailments. Pain in her joints and legs from standing all those years sorting mail. She also had pain in her hands from the arthritis, so she decided she would crochet to help her hands become loose. I can remember all the doilies, hats gloves and toilet paper dolls she made to keep herself limber. Everyone knew what to expect on the next occasion from her. She was so smart and always pushing to learn more, to keep her mind working she would do word puzzles and crosswords to keep herself busy.

Throughout her adult life she was fascinated with our history. As mentioned earlier, her maiden name was Hatfield, of the famous Hatfield and McCoy feud. She was constantly journaling, looking up who begot whom and it was everywhere. I tell you if she had Zoom and anscestry.com we would have had it made. She went at it like a mad woman. But for her that was her enjoyment, her passion. It just plain made her happy to uncover each little pearl of who we were.

As the years progressed she lost both her mother and Cap. She now had nothing much to keep her occupied or engaged. She often said she was to never find another man because they would not be able to catch her. She continued to tout daddy as her one and only sole mate and knew that he was still with her after all these years.

When I started to notice her getting confused it was when she came to visit me in AZ. She had always come to visit me and spend usually a month or so in the warmer weather. She came down one year for Christmas, and I noticed that she was confused as to how to get to the bathroom, she would get lost in the house and call out to me to get her back to where she needed to be. All this happened even though when I had visited her a few months prior at home, she appeared very well oriented and able to navigate her way around, so I thought things were fine and it was just a fluke. Her favorite thing was to walk down to the post office (since her retirement it moved down the bottom) to get her mail, waving at all the cars coming and going. Then she was just fine and now she was not. Confusing.

I started visiting more often and started noting more deterioration in her ability to care for herself. The sun downing started happening with her calling me to tell me to come home for dinner and calling my sister to do the same. We had not lived there in a long time. Fortunately, my sister could retire from her job and move closer to her. She continued to have difficulty remembering things, paying bills twice or not at all, driving to the grocery story multiple times a day and walking to get her mail many times. We knew something was not right and needed to provide more direct support for mommy. She was still very strong, still very independent and still very much her stubborn self, often fighting about something she didn't want to do. We were at a loss as to what to do, who to talk to and what was happening. No one in the immediate area was able to provide us with any hope or support as to how to prevent what happened to my grandmother and her other siblings from progressing with my mommy.

My sister, an absolute angel, eventually moved in with mommy. She could be there for her, be able to make sure she was able to stay at home throughout her journey into the abyss of confusion, irritability, inability eventually to understand basic commands or communicate effectively her wants and needs.

It was a long process, one that lasted over about 10 years. Many times, when I would visit, we would have those Pajama Parties where I cut up her still favorite foods of orange wedges and breaded shrimp with coca cola and watched tv seemingly once again normal. She loved animals and people laughing. She would belly laugh and almost at times I would think it was just like when I was a kid. She was fine...She would be fine. For a while, Mommy realized at times she was having difficulties and would say "oh sh..." and try it again. That eventually went away, and a blank stare took control.

As time went by she stopped walking around, stopped looking at me in her loving acknowledging way, stopped touching my face with her hand to show me that she recognized me and stopped talking to me at all. She had gone but was still there. Still in body but not in mind. I grieved, I wanted to have those Pajama Parties again, I wanted to hear her belly laugh and call my name to come to dinner. It was not to be.

When the time came for her physical death. I was so happy that she was going to be with the "love of her life" finally being able to talk, eat her favorite foods and be with Daddy. God made sure that when it happened it was sudden, no pain nothing drawn out. The lessons I have learned from this amazing INVINCIBLE woman are many but I think the 8 most important are as follows:

1. Love long and hard: life is short never give up on love

2. Be strong as a woman: we can do anything, even if it means asking someone for help

3. Never complain about hard work: It is what makes us human

4. Be faithful to our God no matter what: God has our plan laid out for us

5. Never let them see you sweat: Being strong when it counts matters to others

6. Write it all down....cause ya never know when you might forget: Ever so important

7. Carry a Big hoe or at least a gun! Being from the country does count.

8. Have lots of Pajama Parties: you never know what it is really about just enjoy what you have and when you have it.

About Wendy Elliott

Wendy Elliott is an exceptional business entrepreneur with over two decades of experience in neuroscience healthcare management and executive corporate development. Wendy is also a true believer that you can be on the corporate ladder as well as have an entrepreneurial spirit. Wendy holds multiple advanced degrees, including an MBA with a specialization in healthcare administration and a master's degree in speech language pathology and audiology. Very early on Wendy developed a love for communication and always knew that she was going to have a passion for helping people communicate better.

Wendy as the co-author of Amazon Best-Seller in Women and Business, Fearless, and is building her platform to help others use communication. to gain their independence, find their voice and obtain their goals in their career and/or business.

Today Wendy advocates a leader's need to accelerate performance to drive business execution through powerful communication. She delivers her unique service through one-on-one coaching and group dynamics. Through her consultative approach, backed by rigorous evaluation, she assists professionals to develop strategies to gain influence and credibility, build strong stakeholder relationships, and motivate their employees and teams to drive business strategies forward.

Wendy grew up in rural West Virginia and was raised by her grandparents, who adopted her at an early age. Although she was 1 of a blended sibling kinship of 9, she was raised as an only child. After the traumatic untimely loss of her father (who died at age 49 from a heart attack) when Wendy was 7, her mother became a single parent determined to not be affected by her loss. From this point on, Wendy describes that she embarked upon her life's journey to achieve.

She completed her high school education by age 16 and her first master's degree by age 21. She lives to demonstrate to her mother that their sacrifices paid off. Today a well-respected leader and influencer in her professional realm, Wendy utilizes her professional skills and personal time and assets in her professional roles and as cofounder of a nonprofit organization, Elite Foundation, with a mission to combat human exploitation and provide direct assistance to those in need of finding their voice to succeed.

CHAPTER 5

IN BLOOM

By: Nancy Beer

My name is Nancy I am Forty-Eight, a wife, mom of five, but two live in Heaven, nana to ten grandkids ranging in ages from 1 - 14 and I live IN BLOOM on purpose.

How do we become the people we are?

It was a hot summer day, I was six and had only recently taught myself to swim underwater in the baby pool and graduated to the big pool. That same day, I physically became a victim, but mentally was becoming an addict and absolute protector. It was in a public place, with at least a hundred people but hidden at the same time, under the cover of water and the crowd. Not ever knowing who it was that kept grabbing me in private places, or what direction it was going to come from the next time. I remember thinking, don't take this danger over by where your sister is playing nor, could I get out of the water and lead this person to my mom and baby sister. So, I waited for the adult swim whistle and ran out with everyone else. After hiding in the bathroom long enough for the kids to go back in the water, I went outside, hiding and dodging around cars like you would see on television. I made my way to the playground, that's always been a safe place, right? There were teenagers there, I watched them a while laughing and smoking, they were tough, big and carefree like I needed to be. I thought in my little girl mind that if I was bigger like them, no one could do that stuff to me, make me that scared or put my family in danger. I asked for a cigarette and they laughed but gave it to me. Effectively connecting in my innocent mind and heart, a substance with protection and anxiety. They left, and I couldn't stay there by myself, so I prayed for courage, then went back to the safety of the baby pool, a lesson in itself of "settling for less than."

I was a handful for sure, climbing trees, swinging on grapevines, strategically planning out for days how I would use my mom's big umbrella (because mine was obviously too small for such things), to fly from our front porch, sneaking off for hours in the forest or to cross a railroad trestle over the gorge.

My mom and dad divorced when I was around eight years old. When they were together I have a lot of great memories of Sundays singing together as a family at church, DQ or a picnic afterwards. Working on cars with dad. I am so very thankful to have been brought up in my early years knowing that there was something bigger than us. Someone out there who created us and who loves us enough to be a part of our lives, so we don't have to do life alone. We heard a lot of miracle stories, including this one of my dad's survival from falling on a ten-penny nail. It went through his eye and into his brain. He was actually gone from this side of life and came back in my grandpap Gibbs arms, after pap called out to God vowing to dedicate their lives to spreading light and hope. Dad has had health problems his whole life, but he definitely has lived out for this world that promise. My mom's mother preached and was a strong woman. In her late teens, she was kidnapped and held hostage in the city of Baltimore before gaining her captors trust and eventually running away.

Having these beliefs in a higher power you see doesn't mean you will not go through hard things, it just means you don't go through them alone and you have a supernatural courage, light, help and hope. I also think this connection helps you recognize others whom are sent your way to help you or vice- versa. Although happiness many times eluded me, I've never lived one day not believing in a higher power, a hope of more, that faith gave me courage and hope.

Terrified yet empowered by the need to protect my sisters and my mom, I've attacked from behind on several occasions both of my stepdads to save my mom from being hit again. One day when I was twelve running as fast as I could through a path in the forest, after finding our family portrait with a knife sticking out of it and multiple stab wounds from my stepdad being in a drunken rage. Then stepping in front of the loaded rifle to stop a shot, as my mom pulled out of the long driveway, and all the while, her not knowing that I had come out of the forest and upon the scene.

As children, kids, we think our parents know what they are doing and that they make choices intentionally and with purpose. However, if you come from a background of traumatic events like my mom and her mom before her the chances are, your living on desperation auto pilot. Being a kid, I knew my mom, aunts and the other women that my mom and grandma Juanita helped were victims. That for some reason they couldn't get away but in my child's mind, it would switch back and forth between knowing that and thinking they agreed and were choosing this life no matter what it did to them or even the kids. Over the years, I have heard several women say things like, "yes, he's a creep, touching, looking where and at who he shouldn't but at least he always provides for us" or maybe "no he doesn't provide for us but helps hold me and the kids accountable" or "yes, I know he's usually mean but at least he doesn't beat us." Wait...what? Read that again my friend, and you tell me if it sounds like a life that's safe and would be well enjoyed by you and your kids?

During my early years, I had a close friend, her name is Tammy. I felt normal with her, not poor, not dirty inside or shameful. I love her like a sister and always feel at home instantly in her presence. She would invite me over and I could be just a girl there, I didn't have to be a protector. She, then and many other times, among others over the years, would come along at just the right time.

I felt drawn to the forests of West Virginia and would walk in them for hours alone or with my dog. I had several secret and sacred places to go, a cliff that I would meditate and talk to the universe and dream. Rock city where I would run from rock to rock to trees and back, sort of like parkour if it were in a city setting. It was an amazing way to spend hours for me and it was renewing every time.

I quickly picked up at each new school year the routes I could take to keep hands off me even if it meant being late for class, why didn't I tell, because this was the just the way it was. Then there is the whole matter of shame to add to it. I have made the statement many times to myself and out loud to others when given a compliment on my appearance that "beauty is more of a curse than a blessing" I had learned when to hide, when to fight and when to give in so as not to be hurt anymore. We didn't have the phrase "date rape" coined back then, though getting girls drunk has probably always been a thing. Not that I never chose to drink on my own because I did. My ninth-grade year I moved, staying with a family friend temporarily, and another alcoholic ruled family only this time it was no boy but a man and violent, as his teenage son sobbed loudly in the bathroom because although he wanted to rescue me he was a hostage to fear.

It was to be a birthday celebration day, for the two oldest girls, they were turning 15 and 16. As her mom and stepdad came into the kitchen, the birthday cake was placed on the table. She learned of the positive pregnancy test result from her mom's voice while simultaneously behind her mom, a very large man held a chainsaw above his head that was then slammed through the cake and smashing the table into two pieces. The snapshot of that view and his words that were spoken to this teenage girl were dark, malicious, with rage in his eyes and voice. They didn't really stand out to her right then though planted in her subconscious mind because all she could think now was "I'm free" but they would come back to haunt her for years afterwards.

The hope of something more always trumped the scary, most of her life, she had witnessed the women in her family and others wear bruises and casts from men who were either addicts or just mean and chose to radiate and slam darkness onto the people they were supposed to cherish, protect, teach and provide for. She didn't know then that her mom was going through physical abuse again behind closed doors, and her own traumatic childhood traps, of desperation and depression (that part she would find out later when they reconciled). To the teen, all she wanted was out, so when her mom told her to go, which she thought was probably to protect her, she took her escape.

I left home pregnant within two weeks of turning fifteen. It was November and cold in the mountains of West Virginia. One of my uncles took me in for a while and allowed me to have the couch as my bed. My boyfriend was seventeen at the time and on the weekends, he stayed there with me, using his weekly allowance to buy fuel oil so we wouldn't have to wake up with the ceiling covered in frost when it wasn't a payday week for my uncle.

It is a difficult thing to become emancipated at the age of fifteen and after my son AJ was born we were kind of just here and there. In order to get state help, we went into foster care for a time and a wonderful family with a heart and ministry to help girls like me who had struggles in life either by their own choices or life circumstances. My foster mom's ministry (H.U.G.S), is still helping girls today in Preston County WV, and she remains a source of light and a prayer warrior in my life.

I had an abortion at sixteen after becoming pregnant while on birth control, adding a whole new set of beliefs to who I had now become. The two of us teen parents went our separate ways, remaining friends and he a regular part of his son, AJ's life.

I married and had another son, Christopher four years later and spent the most of the next nine years trying to prove to my husband that he was worthy, though he never did believe it and to myself that I was still worthy enough to have this elusive "something more." I knew without a doubt that these boys were already worthy. Alcohol was the drug of choice to escape in our home and many times this put us around people who were violent when drunk, not beyond shooting at the car my kids and I were in, and like the life I'd lived, except no physical abuse.

I don't tend to look at people as if they are evil, that they hurt their family on purpose, I believe most are just dealing with their own issues and do not realize the deep impact their actions have on others.

When alcohol induced malicious things were spoken in my home on Christmas day to my oldest son who was 9, this put me on a determined search, no more going through the motions, accepting this poverty and victim mentality.

I realized I was co-dependent and had other PTSD traits. I decided to own it and stop pretending like those things didn't exist and that my strength was enough to fix it for everyone. If I didn't somehow take a stand that my sons would likely become one of "those" men so unhappy with life (or stuck from childhood trauma) that they had to drown it in a bottle or another drug of choice to make it tolerable. Therefore, likely providing their own lives and families with the same lifestyle I'd experienced and they were experiencing. With this new knowledge and a renewed hope, I overcame my fear of driving and got my license, GED and started college when I was twenty-five, then picked up my boys and got out of dodge for a fresh start.

I knew how to live a life of defense but not this new safe and happy one. I knew I was crashing and all those years of "fight or flight" were catching up to me. After everyone left for the day I would spend my days either crying uncontrollably or sleeping. I sent my sons to live with their dads and went to fix me, thinking maybe 3- 6 months then reunite, but actually it lasted a year. Though to my oldest son AJ (and in my heart) it was abandonment to the gang activity of Baltimore, and other traumatic events on top of the grief of his mom and brother just gone one day. None of that went as planned, it was a decision of desperation that I wasn't equipped to make.

The boys and I were back together, and I remarried a great guy, Roger and gained the gift of a step daughter, Christine. I spent the next 17 years trying to make up to AJ for that one year, enabling of different kinds became a thing, after a time he added heavy drinking, drugs and heartache.

The first time my son overdosed, he was with people who loved him, they did CPR, brought him back and called 911 but were too afraid to stay at his side however they didn't go far so they could watch over him until help arrived. This last time, it was three days before he was taken to the hospital and then only because I called the police from half way across the country within a half hour of boarding my flight home and said, "my son is in a car in this parking lot, he is dying, and the people will not let him out." I had been sent messages while visiting my son Chris and family saying something was seriously wrong with AJ, then ignored by the sender. I called 911 and it was cancelled, afterward I was told that he refused, but that had to be a lie because he couldn't talk or walk. As it turned out, the peace I had been given during an intense prayer, that had stalled me from calling family members to go rescue him, the day before was correct. In hindsight all the pieces came together to save his life. The top surgeon in the USA that specializes in this type of drug overdose leading to brain hemorrhages arrived that third day for a lecture. Had he not been there to confer, protocol would've opened him up to relieve the swelling and it was inoperable. My husband Roger was also given this same peace after hours of prayer plus an angelic experience that one day maybe we can share.

Watching my son come back into who he was before I left him at twelve was a beautiful thing. He was hope filled and excited about life. After a massive brain bleed, the sac around his heart started bleeding, thirty days in the hospital, the right side of his body not working fully, he walked away with a heart, mind and soul that no longer held any bitterness from life's traumatic events and his own choices.

Unfortunately, after three months of healing, AJ walked back into that addict world to try to help bring someone out, got stuck again himself. A lot of hate was spewed at our family and I went into a dark place that I'd never been before. I knew that I couldn't stay there because it's not who I am made to be.

So, what can you do?

Add as much light as you possibly can that's what and get as many others to come along with you as you can. Contemporary Christian music and singing through that storm was what started bringing me out. I also decided to go into home health because I needed to go do something meaningful. It worked for me, thank God because I could've ended up in jail or worse taking up an addiction myself to hide, because I considered several options.

We did an intervention and AJ successfully completed a year and half of drug rehab. While he still has health issues, some of which include seizures, sleep walking, thalamic pain syndrome that we haven't been able to control along with right side of the body deficit, we now can focus on physical and cognitive therapy, with the new neurology team on board we have high hopes.

I still struggle with what I assume is a type of survivor guilt when I read or hear of other mothers, whose child didn't survive. God is not done with me yet, even though this bad thing happened, we are going to use it for good.

My missions:

Add FREE self-defense classes in schools for underprivileged kids and courses about inappropriate sexual behavior, both starting in kindergarten.

Help parents recognize when in dysfunctional home, your child's perception (NOT YOURS) is their total reality, it becomes part of them and they may not have the strength or hope to bring themselves out healthy, happy and whole if they survive it that is because some don't. I know because I was that kid, so was my mom, her mom and my kids.

Hope is alive that is for sure, but we must be determined to search it out and keep it forefront. If you have been stuck for so very long, like I was, please know my friend that FREEDOM IS CALLING YOUR NAME!

What legacy do you want to leave here on this planet?

What legacy will you leave, on purpose?

Special thanks to Jesus, my Savior also my son Christopher Cole, for always encouraging and not letting me settle any longer only being, who I thought I was.

Thank You AJ Pell for letting me write about you, also to those who helped me throughout the hemorrhagic stroke time: Roger, Gwenda, David, Mary, Tammy, Pastor Kelly, Samantha, Ruth, Pell Family, John-Erik, my IW team, WPER, ROLWC, and Elite Foundation Inc.

May God bless all you put your hands and heart to do,

Nancy Beer

About Nancy Beer

Nancy Beer is the mother of three children and grandmother of ten. She and her husband Roger enjoy life on a piece of the Virginia forest with their fur babies Punk & Roxy.

Currently a Health Care Professional.

She runs from her phones two successful Network Marketing companies.

One is a company that is at the forefront of Nutrigenomics by biohacking the aging code, check it out here:

http://lifebiohacked.com

The other monitoring your own health with advanced real time Wearable Technology, and Biozen to reduce EMF radiation from your electronic devices.

NancyBeer.WORLDgn.com

Go find her on FB and see what it means to Live IN BLOOM!

Facebook.com/Nancy.s.beer

CHAPTER 6

KINTSUKUROI

By: Melissa Binkley

"We all do the best with what we can, when we know how and

when we know better, we do better." ~ Binkley

I want to take you on a journey from who I was, to the awakening of who I AM. It started in my infancy, but I will start this story from a later time in my life, when I became enlightened by the wisdom found in the art of Kintsukuroi

Kintsukuroi, an art form that literally means, "to repair with gold." It is a way of living that embraces every flaw and imperfection. The idea that something that has been broken is more valuable and beautiful because of its brokenness and not in spite of it.

In the tea houses of Japan when a ceramic pot or bowl would break, an artisan would lovingly restructure the piece using gold or silver lacquer, to create something stronger and more beautiful than it was before. The breaking was not something to hide, but instead something to celebrate and cherish. In the repair, the bowl becomes a work of art that is more valuable than it was before. Once repaired it took on a life of its own from its, "rebirth."

The rebirth, provides a new sense of purpose, vitality, and resilience raising appreciation to even greater heights. The true life of the bowl begins the moment it is dropped, "So it is not simply any mended object that increases in its appreciation but...the gap between the vanity of pristine appearance and the fractured manifestation of mortal fate deepens its appeal." In other words, it is the proof of its resilience and fragility that truly makes it beautiful.

I have spent the last several years crossing the globe and in my humbling travels, I have seen more trauma and more love than I could ever have imagined. I am always in awe of humanity and its resilience and I bow to our ability to transform and heal. I once heard someone say, "You can never truly heal from your trauma." I will let you decide if that is the truth or a false belief perpetuated throughout our society as a way to entrench us in even more trauma and fear.

It was 1996, I stood posing nude in broad daylight on the streets of Annapolis, Maryland with my photographer, when five young Naval Academy men strolled by in their dress blues, feeling thankful that the bite marks I usually scared my arms with were not visible but grateful that my ribs were sticking through my starving body, it didn't take much convincing to allow a naked 19-year-old lie across their outstretched arms. You see, it was the Perfect picture in my attempt to be a perfect 10. I always wanted to be a perfect 10, or so I thought. In my late teens, I even tried to get accepted into the popular men's magazine, Perfect 10, by photographing "artistic" nudes, as a way of getting the love and validation, I so desperately craved then.

"We will seek outside what we are never shown is already residing within." ~ Binkley

It wasn't until the age of forty that I realized I was a ten and had been since my childhood. I was a ten out of ten for Adverse Childhood Experiences (ACE Score). An ACE score is like a report card for abuse and neglect experienced before you turn 18; and like my high school report card I had gotten all A's on the ACE! As I read the ACE 10 questions and slowly checked off, yes for each one, I came to the true realization of my *kintsukuroi*. My ability to be broken and fragile and repair my life with resilience, purpose and healing, and the golden lacquer that has made it all the more valuable, rich and beautiful. Each of us has a wound that has broken us so deeply that the only way to repair it is with gold. In the process of mending you never believe that you can truly heal, that you will be grateful for the tragedy, that you can in turn make it your greatest gift. Not only do you not believe it, you know it is not impossible. Until one day you find your first crumb of hope that turns into the golden flecks that become an experience of true gratitude. Gratitude for the trauma. Your Traumitude!

Just like the bowl whose true life begins when it is first broken, and as mine began when I was first broken. My heart, my mind, and body are covered in golden lacquer. Although I don't remember the first time, my true life began while I was in the womb, for I wasn't even meant to be born, a regression in my 30's took me there and I remembered what I didn't know, that I was nearly beaten to death before I even took my first breath. From that moment forward, I remember the countless nights of terror as I huddled in my room watching my mother be pulled across the room by her hair or hearing the screams of agony. At the age of nine, I became mother, caretaker and solace for my two younger sisters, as our mother was taken from us. She was alive but gone, escaped to save herself from abuse. By the time I was 10, I was left alone with my 4-year-old sister in an empty apartment with no furniture and cockroaches. Without food I was left to get nourishment from the neighbors, a married couple with an infant girl. The mother was gone, the baby was in the high chair, but they had food and TV! I thought this was surely heaven. Until he asked me to lie down on his chest and as I watched the TV show I felt his hands down my pants. I panicked, my little sister sat on the floor, what would he do to her, if I said anything. It took me 17 years to tell anyone and I carried the guilt with me all that time. In my mind, I caused harm to that little baby girl because I never told anyone. It was in that moment I learned to be silent. And, that is was safer to not speak up and just do what others wanted.

I spent many nights that year alone, with no father or mother, to care for me. My hair was never combed, and my clothes were dirty when I went to school, I had no idea how to take care of myself and I was severely shy and angry. So, I read books. Lots of books. 1000-page adult books, when I was only in 4th grade. I was teased and quickly became suicidal. It was a cold winter night when finally, a knock came to the door and my grandpa said he had had enough and took me and my sister home with him.

Then on a cold December night in 1994, vying for Valedictorian of my high school, joining every sport that was offered and seemingly living a normal teenage life, I was locked in a garage and brutally raped by a man 10-years my senior. I was a senior in high school, seemingly with my life ahead of me, but my life came to a screeching halt. The bowl that was my life completely shattered unable to hold its shape any longer and it took more than 15 years before I started to mend it and find Traumitude. I spent countless days numb, staring blankly out a window listlessly doing puzzles and waiting for the school year and the rape trial to end. I would have never believed it, that someday, this moment would be my flagship of Traumitude.

Traumitude means the utmost gratitude for your traumatic experiences, the modern-day version of *kintsukuroi*, meaning to repair what only appeared to be shattered with the golden realization of your truth to heal.

Within six years of my graduation from Waynesfield-Goshen, I had gotten married and divorced, had a beautiful daughter, Michayla, graduated from The Ohio State University, obtained and lost a corporate job, learned to hide my eating disorder and self-mutilation behind fitness regimens, became a regular drug user and a full-time drug dealer. I knew how to pretend that everything was OK. I never spoke about my trauma, to the contrary, I would have told you I had "fixed" it all. I had burned my court case papers in an amalagana fire, and the nightmares no longer haunted me nightly. The endless supply of drugs and parties allowed me to easily hide my trauma in a beautiful box with a bow and pretend it didn't exist.

But I knew it was there every time I returned home. Every time I entered the town I would feel anger, sadness, and rage would build up inside me for what was lost and taken. The house with the garage I had been raped in sat directly across from the house my grandpa had rescued me from so many years earlier. It catty cornered the Minnich's grocery store with my family name that my grandparents had owned and run until I was a teenager. The invisible triangle that connected those three places from my youth were like the Bermuda triangle. Enter and you may be lost forever. When I drove into the triangle of terror on subsequent travels "home" I knew I was not fixed. I could feel the black endless hole that I was slowly dragging my life and body into. I never believed I could escape or that I would ever truly heal. I would hold up my double middle fingers and say, "Fuck You!" before driving on.

"It is not what happens to you that matters, it is what you do with it that defines your life."

I was on a whirlwind of destruction by 2004, quickly heading to one of two places: the grave or prison. I now realize that the synchronistic and magical events that saved me from myself so many times was not luck or chance but my Intuitive Intelligence hitting me over the head like a 2 x 4 to awaken me, to my possibilities.

In the basement of my large mansion like home in German Village I had a secret room. The walls of this room were white but not from the plaster, rather from a fine dust of cocaine that had built up over the previous year, from the grinding and rerocking of coke with a 12-ton press. Suddenly one night something terribly scared me, and I called in a couple of people to dismantle the press and take it away. This one small act would save me years in prison when a tragedy occurred at my home only weeks later.

I barely escaped Ohio in 2004 with my life intact as I ran away to Florida, leaving behind my 6-year-old daughter. When you are not strong enough to save yourself, there is always a force there offering its support to show you the way to your greatness. That force was the love and connection I had for my daughter. It was my incessant love for her and my belief that we had shared many lifetimes that moved me towards saving myself. I only came to know later it was my connection to something greater than me that would change everything.

In 2004, I began to dig my way out. It felt like I had been dropped in a massive well and I was using my bare hands to scratch my way to the top. I spent five years trying to heal, thinking I was "doing" the right things. My body was sick from food disorders, exercise disorders and drugs. Then in 2009, I had my first real breakthrough. I stopped fighting myself and finally asked for guidance and help beyond my conscious capabilities. This action landed me with an eviction notice and bouncing from car to friends' homes for nearly a year. I had asked for this and what ensued was the journey to I AM. It was the moment when my heart was sewn back together and pulled apart, at the same time. It was my experience of the golden thread of humanity, the Japanese ceramic bowls that have been reclaimed and lacquered with golden lace. A journey from broken and homeless to whole and fulfilled, serving as an international leader, speaker, and spiritual teacher for thousands.

This journey to Intuitive Intelligence became my sacred revolution. It is not the situation or the event but the lack of trust in ourselves that rattles us. It is the betrayal of our own identity and beliefs that truly shake us to the core. This is when the opportunity to completely shift and transform comes. When you are stripped of everything and must build from the ground, starting with trusting yourself first. You always knew the answers, and you refused to listen.

Before every breakthrough there is a breakdown. You must break down old beliefs, ideas, and habits to ascend to a new existence.

I spent years breaking the habit of being me, that little girl that never grew up, the soul that had chosen this. I could never lead and teach without having been in the darkness. To be the lighthouse shining through the darkness you must first understand it, cherish it, love it and hold it. Otherwise you will always judge it and those in it. Sacred revolution comes when you can not only let go of judgement and fear but accept even the enemy and forgive.

Realizing that forgiveness really doesn't exist because why would you ever forgive your greatest spiritual teachers.

I slowly began to heal and as I healed I helped others to do the same and I built it into a business. I was living proof of *kintsukuroi*, broken I had seemed to lose my honor, yet in my brokenness I had the ability to gain a whole new level of appreciation through my mending. So was I ever truly broken? I was becoming stronger, more beautiful and more resilient than I was before.

In 2010, I began training at the Institute for Integrative Nutrition (IIN) to learn to truly heal my body from years of abuse and to get a plan and system to help others like me. In 2017, I was asked to return to IIN to teach *Intuitive Intelligence*. I had come full circle. I painstakingly went from homeless to hopeful and by November 2014, after my first conference, I made a seemingly crazy decision to start traveling the world, speaking, and sharing my message.

That year I said I would be international by 2016 and promised my daughter that I would take her backpacking through Europe for her graduation gift the same year. At that point in my life I had just come off of my first Pure BodyLove conference which had literally bankrupted me, although I had had my highest paying year up until then (at least legally) and had tripled my income from 2013.

Not only did I not have a passport in 2014 when I made this decision, I was denied it earlier in the year when I applied because I was $15,000 in arrears in child support. The arrears occurred, one from being homeless and jobless in 2009 and two from being a struggling wanna-be entrepreneur up until that year.

At that moment in 2014, I decided to follow my inner voice. I gave up my home in February 2015 and started traveling and spent the next 33 months travelling. The child support was taken care of by November of 2015 and in April of 2016 I received my passport.

In 2016, exactly 20 years after the experience that had completely shattered my bowl of life I returned to my alma mater, Waynesfield-Goshen. My daughter, whom I had a deep and loving relationship with, was a senior in high school. She had a track meet at my old school and I was headed home to face my past. It had been 13 years since my last visit. I had made a promise to my daughter to attend as many of her Senior Year functions as possible, so I flew in to Columbus, rented a car and drove to Waynesfield.

As I drove into the same spot, my Bermuda triangle, I turned off the car. I stared at the battered and worn-down building that used to be Minnich's grocery. I looked at my father's old home, and my eyes landed on THE garage. I brought my hands in prayer to my quivering lips and I cried tears of joy, under my breath as I said, "Thank You" over and over. My triangle of torment had become my triangle of triumph. This became my place of the deepest Traumitude.

As I sat there the realization that my greatest spiritual growth had come in the wake of much; love and loss; trauma and forgiveness; falling in love and mending broken hearts; waiting for courage and being vulnerable; and Becoming bitter before surrendering to a new path. The path of Intuitive Intelligence, of spiritual leadership, an awakening to my truth.

I took Michayla to five countries in Europe and spoke in London at a conference that summer and continued my travels for another year. I ended up in places such as India to speak in front of 2000 and in Southeast Asia. I spent a month in Nepal in 2017, serving women and teaching Traumitude and Intuitive Intelligence. That same year, I opened the doors to the Intuitive Intelligence Academy and began teaching these processes to others, so that they too could heal their own trauma, connect to their Intuitive Intelligence, and learn how to do this work for themselves, as well as share it with their communities and tribes so together we can reach One billion people in my lifetime.

What you seek is always waiting for you, and it is your duty to go find it and create your *kintsukuroi.*

About Melissa Binkley

Melissa Binkley is a humanitarian and activist on a mission to help society to transcend through trauma to a new level of consciousness. She is the creator and founder of The Intuitive Intelligence Academy™. She is Intuitive Intelligence™ Trainer, Certified Mastery Transformational Coach, Soul & Business Strategist, #1 Best- Selling Author. Melissa is a dynamic, highly sought-after International Speaker and Thought Leader known for her ability to transcend limiting beliefs, she uses several techniques that fuse science and spirituality, personal development, and the quantum field.

In 2014, Melissa developed her own mode of Spiritual Transformational Process called Intuitive Intelligence™ that is changing the way coaches, healers, and speakers connect with their audiences and transform lives and heal trauma through this new healing modality. Melissa is on a mission to raise social, sustainable, conscious awareness and spirituality through a wholistic approach through supporting healers, creatives, artists, light-workers, highly-sensitive coaches and speakers to live their purpose, tap into Intuitive Intelligence™ to create a Global Impact.

She believes you can curse, have tattoos, own guns, dance till dawn and still be spiritual. Exotic countries, Yoga, hiking, and Green Matcha Lattes light her up. She intends to raise the vibration of 1 billion people and heal trauma through her humanitarian work. Melissa is a sought after speaker who has share the stage with Marianne Williamson and Dr. John Demartini and is also a teacher for the Institute for Integrative Nutrition teaching Intuitive Intelligence and Speaking and on the Advisory Committee for the Woman's Economic Forum. To find out more information visit MelissaBinkley.com,UniteSummit.org,

or IntuitiveIntelligenceAcademy.com or reach out personally to Melissa at melissa@melissabinkley.com.

CHAPTER 7

MY YELLOW BRICK ROAD TO HOLLYWOOD

By: Chloë Bellande

Have you ever wanted something so bad that it hurts?

Just like GERD, the feeling had me in chronic pain from the very first day I put on my high school uniform. I was the youngest and shortest of my class, the quiet type and the perfect prey for bullies. My teachers would always report me as, "being distracted during class," because I had attention disorder, so my mother strongly encouraged extracurricular activities in the hopes that I'd become more socialized.

In 7th grade, I had to write a short play for my theater class. When we presented it to our student body, to my surprise, the play was critically acclaimed. That moment, something magical happened. The kind of awe and delight that the students had in my story made me realize that I had the power to move people. That feeling translated into a sense that all is right with the world; and all is right in *my* world. My interest in writing drifted from theater to film, after I wrote my very first screenplay that summer. I no longer felt the need to fit in, just a burning desire to achieve what I wanted most in my life: telling stories that entertain, inspire and change the world.

Of course, entering the adult world, I realized that my yellow brick road to Emerald City would have a lot of potholes.

After I got my Associate degree, I applied to Concordia University, which was at the time, the *only* affordable school in my town with a film program. To my dismay, I was rejected outright without explanation. I didn't have the financial means to study abroad, so during the 4 years that followed, I was pursuing my studies in Arts and Languages, and I kept re-applying to the film program every year. When that last rejection letter arrived, I went straight to the Dean's office and demanded that he reconsider his decision. I still remember his exact words, as they haunted me for weeks after I left his office, "*You are too mainstream, and you don't have what it takes to be a film major.*" I was heartbroken, confused, and as much as I replayed that scene in my head, all I could process was, "*You are not good enough.*" So I did what any tenacious girl would do, I decided to prove him wrong.

After my graduation, I took independent film workshops to learn about camera angles and how to use professional editing software. Then, I wrote a screenplay and made my directorial debut with, 'Battle of Souls', a self-financed feature film that I produced on a shoestring budget with the help of other aspiring filmmakers and first-time actors.

This led to my first official selection by a film festival in Hollywood. Flash forward to the day we first stepped on the red carpet at the Sunset 5 Theater. It was a beautiful summer day. We met Kristanna Loken (Terminator 3: Rise of The Machines), as her film, 'Lime Salted Love' was premiering at the festival. We also met legendary actor Dick Van Dyke who was starring in a documentary, The Wonder Kids. The real Disney magic was when we were told that our movie had won Best Feature Film (Thriller), beating all the amazing other movies in the same category. I felt like a CHAMPION.

My thirst for knowledge in my dream career kept growing. Every time I had a chance, I took days off from my day job and travelled to attend screenwriting workshops and seminars to work on my craft.

After a few years of procrastination, I went on and produced another movie, 'While the Village Sleeps'. This was a gift that kept on giving. I won my first Best Screenplay award at an Academy Award Qualifying film festival, the movie trailer was selected at the Hollywood Discovery Awards, and, I attended the 16th Hollywood Film Awards, a star-studded gala where I was literally sitting across the table from the cast of the Avengers. I was officially star-stuck! The cherry on the cake was when I got accepted to screen my movie at the 66th Cannes Film Festival at the Short Film Corner, a non-competitive section giving opportunities to filmmakers to showcase their work. Mingling and networking with industry professionals taught me so much more about the business than any film school could. I was ready to dive into the world of professional storytellers. I felt unstoppable...

Unfortunately, like in every story, there is a moment where the hero and the villain finally meet.

Living in a small town with very little opportunities to thrive in my chosen career, it was time for me to step up my game and plant some seeds in a bigger pot. Ironically, Will Of Fortune, my 3rd movie, was the game-changer in my journey as I decided to shoot it in New York City, the land of opportunities.

I spent a couple of months travelling to New York on the weekends for the movie's pre-production and riding the Greyhound bus back to Montreal on Sundays, so I could get back to my day-job on Monday mornings. On a cold February evening, I hopped on the bus to go meet with my production crew in New York for what was supposed to be our last day on set. When we stopped at the US Port of entry, the Border Patrol questioned my motives for visiting the United States, this time around. I told him the truth because I didn't think I was doing anything wrong. I was immediately escorted back to the bus where I had to grab my luggage while being starred at by 60 pair of judging eyes, and then back to the office where I was practically treated like a criminal.

I've had mug shots and fingerprints taken and a never-ending interrogation, just like in the movies with an officer playing "good cop, bad cop" in a plain room with nothing but a table. Apparently, a Canadian shooting a film in the United States without a special permit was considered performing illegal work on American soil, and therefore, against Federal law. After nearly 4 hours of emotional torture, the officer drove me back to the Canadian border in a law enforcement truck. Once there, I had to sit outside and wait for a bus going back to downtown Montreal.

I finally got home in the morning, and my roommate, Nadia, had just woken up. She asked, "So why are you still here?" I told her what had happened. I had no answer. My brain was frozen and couldn't get passed the idea that I had people waiting for me at Grand Central Station in New York, probably worried by now. She told me with conviction because she believed in me and that my movie could still happen, "Go back and try another Port of Entry!" As much as it sounded like a bad idea, Nadia was right. I couldn't sit there and process. I HAD to find a way to finish that movie while the clock was ticking.

After I got off the phone with my Production Manager who had suggested that we cancel the production until further notice, I had a crazy idea that might work, and I needed him to trust me. After running a few tests, we decided to give it a shot.

The next morning, while the whole crew was on set in New York, my Production Manager was pointing his smartphone's camera to give me a view of the scene and I was calling the shots from Skype. The Wi-Fi connection was flickering, and we had a 15 second delay on the image.

We barely got by, but thanks to the help of my Director of Photography and my Producer who both took over whenever I couldn't see the shot, we laboriously wrapped the production that day. They mailed me the footage on a hard drive, so I could edit and complete the movie.

Three months later, 'Will of Fortune' premiered at the Cannes Film Festival's Short Film Corner, and was a Top Finalist for Best Screenplay in 4 script competitions. However, that victory was short-lived as I was subsequently declined entrance in the United States, again, that summer. Only this time, the Border Patrol filed a report stating that I was permanently banned from visiting the United States unless I had a waiver or a Visa. She kept asking me the same questions over and over, convinced that I was hiding evidence of a possible ongoing film project. I explained that I was just visiting friends for the weekend, but the more I talked, the more I would get myself out of the frying pan into the fire. I was fed up and exhausted. I had enough.

While I was sitting outside waiting for my ride home, the woman who had officially ruined my weekend stepped out and handed me a pile of papers and told me, "you're pretty successful in your field", in a tone that sounded vaguely confusing. I didn't have any interest in conversing with her, especially after the heart wrenching turmoil I had just endured, so I grabbed the sheets and gave a quick look. She had Googled me and photocopied everything she found, including a page of instructions on how to get a work permit for artists and performers. She told me, "You have great credentials; you should try applying for a Visa." I gave her a dismissive look and she left, smiling as if she was on to something.

The following days, I had a reality-check consultation with an immigration lawyer. According to him, a work Visa would require an employer's sponsorship – which I would never get thanks to the dent in my file describing me as a federal offender. The Green card I wanted was a self-petition based on extraordinary abilities and did not require any employer's sponsorship.

My lawyer asked, "What are your backups? Maybe thinking there was a chance I could get a Visa through marriage or other means. I responded with determination, "I don't need a backup. I'm getting the Green Card. In fact, not only did I not fully qualify to apply, but that category had a 99% rejection rate and was usually granted to workers already established in the United States. Let's pause for a second.

This is the part where the hero doubts his own powers after hitting a brick wall. Cue in the nostalgic song with a montage showing the hero trying to get back to what society calls a normal life. Oh! And don't forget the voices of the naysayers with limited beliefs telling him why his plan would have never worked, and that he is much better off in the comfort zone, away from all disappointments.

But wait. What if that hero did **not** choose the life he was given? What if his life chose **him**?

And that's when it hit me.

Great power comes with great responsibility. People with regular lives may have that option; but heroes don't get to quit. Dreamers don't get to settle for an uneventful life. A dream is a purpose, and a purpose *must* be fulfilled to live a meaningful life.

I snapped out of my Spider-Man moment and started working on my next move. I refused to believe that my story was going to end here, stranded in my hometown, with no physical access to the one place that had proven to give more opportunities in the entertainment industry than any other country in the world. That brick wall would have to fall or else I was going to carve out a door and break it open.

The next months were challenging. I quit my job, decluttered my life, got rid of all my furniture and moved back home. I was glued to my laptop 50 hours per week, and when I wasn't starring at a screen, I was out networking, collaborating, getting involved in different projects within my capacity until my list of Green card eligibility criteria was completely checked-off.

I called my lawyer when I was ready to apply. It had been exactly 12 months since our initial conversation. Not only did I fully qualify but I managed to scrap enough money to pay for the entire process. When my application was sent, I crossed out every calendar day until the morning I received an email from the USCIS.

Picture this: I had no job offer, no money, no family sponsorship or an American husband, just this one-time chance; and all I needed was one word and my whole life would turn around. I took a deep breath and read the email.

My Green card application was APPROVED.

For the very first time in my life, I was speechless. I had no word to express the ecstatic emotion I was feeling. Every part of my body wanted to burst in excitement. God had answered my prayers. Despite everybody's expectations, I had broken all the rules and won the game. Finally, I understand the meaning of "everything happens for a reason".

Being rejected from film school gave me the drive that I needed to produce my first film. Getting hands-on experiences provided me with knowledge of my craft that I applied on the projects that followed, and that's how I went from red tape to red carpets. Being declined entrance in the United States was a blessing in disguise. God had temporarily taken away what I "wanted" and forced me to work harder so I could get what I "needed." For a headstrong and stubborn person like myself, big moves are only made when the circumstances force me to.

When we face roadblocks, in the end, it all comes down to the choices that we make. No matter the size of the curveballs, we always have the choice to either accept it and make the best out of it, or, step forward and change it. That is our *only* job. The only thing we really have control on.

A new day begun on the morning I packed and moved to Hollywood, leaving behind everything and everyone I've ever known. Mixed feelings of eagerness and anxiety invaded my mind while I was headed to the "unknown" – a new world of possibilities has yet to be fully explored. Amidst the complexity of my relocation and the rollercoaster of emotions that I had to overcome, in my darkest nights, these thoughts would lift up my spirit in trust and hope to find the pot of gold at the end of the rainbow: "Limits don't exist. We only see them because we blindly believe the skeptical, and by doing so, we create our own limitations, our own fears. But if we keep walking in faith, trusting the *invisible*, we *can* be heroes; we can become *invincible*".

About Chloe Bellande

Chloë Bellande is a Screenwriter and Film Director of crime dramas and thrillers. Her film festival acclaimed movies While The Village Sleeps, and, Will Of Fortune have won several awards and nominations for the Best Screenplay and Best Movie Trailer. She was born in Montreal, Canada, and while in her hometown, she experimented with various occupations: Montreal Times weekly paper columnist, Radio host, freelance video editor, office clerk...But writing has always been her passion.

In 2016, she won the Canada Latin Awards for Best Director/Producer for her sustained achievements in the entertainment industry. She relocated to Los Angeles, California after receiving a permanent residency based on her Extraordinary Abilities in Motion Pictures and TV. Today Chloë is living out her dream-life as an entreprenuer in the film industry and is giving back through her role with Elite Foundation, as Elite's Production silo Manager.

CHAPTER 8

VICTIM TO VICTOR

By: Samantha Parma-Vera

My name is Samantha Alexandra Parma-Vera and I refuse to be seen as a victim! This is the sentence that I would repeat to myself whenever I struggled to remember that the horrible things that were done to me did not define who I was but made me stronger.

This story begins when a naïve, 15-year-old me started playing around on social media and chatting with random boys from all over Florida. I was so hungry for attention that I resorted to searching the virtual world to find it. My phone screen was my safety barrier; or so I thought. It wasn't long before I started getting chat requests from different boys but there was one boy whom I spent most of my time. He was a cute 15-year-old boy that gave me just the right amount of attention to have me wound tightly around his finger. We communicated back and forth for a pretty long time (which was about a week or two) before he started asking to meet in person. At first, I was hesitant, but eventually he had asked so many times that I finally agreed to meet him at our neighborhood mall. We had planned it all out and the date was set. It was at this time that my mother started to notice that I was very secretive and withdrawn, so she took all of my electronic devices away. She already had access to all my phone data and took it upon herself to find out what I had really been doing locked up in my room away from the real world. If my mother had not made that decision, I probably wouldn't be here sharing my story with you. My mother was able to gain access into the back portal of the app and see whom I was really talking to. It turned out that the cute 15-year-old boy I had been in communication with was actually a 50-year-old registered pedophile and human trafficker that was grooming me for the sex trade. This was a major wake-up call that actually led me to get involved in human trafficking awareness. But unfortunately, over the next few years I hit road bump after road bump.

Like many other teenagers, I had major self-esteem issues and craved the attention of men because I thought that their opinions of me determined my self-worth. I now know where these issues stemmed from but unfortunately, I learned too late. Fast-forward two years; I'm now 17 and attending a new school in my junior year of high school. High school really was never my thing, so I felt completely displaced in this new environment, but I tried to make it through. Fortunately, I wasn't the only new kid coming into the school at an awkward time. This was when I met my first "real" boyfriend. We were both outcasts, so we immediately hit it off and eventually started dating. It was all sunshine and butterflies to begin with but as the relationship progressed it started to become very unhealthy and he began to show his true colors. I was very co-dependent on him and again found myself wrapped around another man's finger. He knew this to be true and used it to his advantage. He was verbally and mentally abusive and ultimately alienated me from my family. I had lost who I was but more importantly my parents didn't know who I was anymore. My parents decided to intervene again as they saw what I couldn't see at the time. I remember sitting on my bed after being busted for sneaking out to see him and my parents coming into my room and telling me that they were sending me away to a bible college in Europe. As you can imagine, at the time I resented my parents for sending me away because I saw it more as a punishment versus a way of saving me. That trip ultimately changed my life and made me realize how toxic of a relationship I was involved. Upon returning home I ended all connections with this man and continued my life. I was finally happy and content with how much progress I had made but unfortunately that all came tumbling down.

Shortly after ending my previous relationship, I met what I thought was a great Christian boy during my senior year of high school, who was going to attend my selected university. We really hit it off and not too long later started dating. I really thought that I had found a great guy that respected me and would never manipulate me. We dated all throughout our senior year and eventually went off to university together. The university that we went to was out-of-state, so it was our first taste of true "independence." We were like a married couple and had even talked about getting married after school. Everything was going so well, and I was genuinely happy. As time went on, we started making more and more friends and getting invited to all kinds of events. We were inseparable and would go with each other everywhere. One night we got invited to a party at an upper-classman's loft. There was music, lots of people and a lot of alcohol. That was not my first experience with alcohol, but it was my first experience with "jungle juice," and I had a few too many cups. For those of you that don't know, "jungle juice" is a concoction of three parts mixed alcohol and one-part juice. Due to the amount of sugar in the juice you can't really taste the alcohol so one cup turned into two, which then turned into three or four. I had underestimated the potency of the juice and became very drunk. It was at this time that we finally decided to leave as I started to get sick. Once back at our friend's home, he took care of me and when I was finally done throwing up he put me to bed. Things were getting pretty fuzzy at that point, but I will never forget what happened next.

At the beginning of our relationship, we had decided to stay abstinent but after going away to university sex became a very big topic. I explained my reasons for staying pure and truly thought that he understood and respected my decision. But as I lay almost unresponsive on that bed, I remember him undressing me and touching my body and then getting undressed himself. In my head, I was saying 'No,' 'Stop,' 'Don't,' but the words just wouldn't come out of my mouth. I was frozen and then it happened. It was at this point that I went completely numb and allowed myself to drift away. The next morning, I remember getting up to use the restroom and just being in pain. I could not accept what had happened to me. I blocked the images out of my brain from the previous night and continued as nothing had ever happened. We continued dating for several months after that until I decided to transfer back to Florida. It was then, once he was out of my life that everything came crashing down. At the time, I didn't know that you could be raped by a significant other. When I finally decided to face what had happened to me it was like the flood gates came crashing down and I was completely overwhelmed with so many emotions. I was raped and sodomized by someone I trusted, and thought loved me.

After a few months passed, I decided that I was going to confront him on what he did. At first, he was apologetic and remorseful, but he then tried to shift the blame to me. Saying that it was my fault and that I wanted it. That was the last day I ever talked to him. From that point on it all just went downhill.

My mom knew that something was up with me, as I was not myself during that time. I was depressed, angry, confused and completely withdrawn from the world around me. I would go to school, work and then lock myself in my room. One day my mom decided that we were going for a drive and talk. She started asking me what was wrong, why I wasn't myself and if something had happened to me. It was at that moment that I basically lost my shit, for lack of better words. As I was sobbing and shaking uncontrollably I told her what had happened to me while away at university. She just held me as I let out every emotion that I had hid for so long. When I finally started to calm down we started to take apart the past four years of my life to understand the root cause of what triggered all my toxic behaviors. It all came down to another incident that happened when I was 15-years-old. It was the day that my parents found out that I had lost my virginity. I decided that I was going to lose my virginity at an away-regatta to a guy that was on my rowing team. When we came back from the race I remember being called to the coach's office and being told that I was kicked off the team due to the decision I made, as I signed a contract that stated that I could not be in a guy's room. I never imagined the repercussions that would follow my decision. I threw away the chance to be the youngest female on the team to race at nationals, I got kicked off the team and I had to tell my parents why I was kicked off the team. I thought the hardest part was going to be telling my parents, but it was what happened after that was the hardest to deal with. After I told my parents, my dad looked me in eyes with anger and called me a whore and a slut. My heart shattered. He later apologized and said he never meant it and I thought I had forgiven him, but those words stayed in the back of my mind from that point on. In the years that followed I had what people nowadays call "daddy issues."

But don't worry this story has a good ending. In the past year, I have been able to completely change my life around and learn from my past experiences. My dad and I have the best relationship now and his words no longer haunt me. I'd be lying if I told you that I was completely healed; but if I've learned anything it's that this is not a sprint, it's a marathon. It's going to take time to be completely back to normal and that is totally ok. You can't expect to do a total 360 from one day to the next. I can also tell you that it's not going to be easy. You're going to have good days and you're going to have bad days. But when you do have bad days you need to put on your big girl pants and keep pushing through. The things that you have experienced do NOT determine whether you are a victim. Only YOU can decide whether you are a victim or a victor. You need to take back control of your life and keep moving forward. If you don't think that you can do it on your own, put aside your pride and ask for help. That is one thing that I still struggle with and am still learning to do. I never asked for help in the past because I thought that I could deal with it on my own, but the reality was that at the beginning I was too weak to do it on my own. There is no shame in asking for help; it only goes to show that you recognize that you cannot do it by yourself. Sometimes to move forward you need a crutch for support. Surround yourself with people that you know would support you through anything. Having a close group of friends that have your back and encourage you can make your journey a little bit easier. From the experiences that I have had thus far, I can assure you that keeping it bottled in is the absolute worst thing you can possibly do. You need to talk about it, learn from it and let it go. I know that this all sounds harsh, but the reality is that this journey is not all rainbows and unicorns. I can tell you from my own experience that it has been the hardest journey but by pushing through I have come out on the other side as the victor. However, you also need to understand now that this is a life-long journey. But once you stop seeing yourself as the victim it only gets easier.

When my mom asked me to join the group of authors that are writing in this book I was a bit hesitant at first. I wasn't sure, if I was ready to share these traumatic parts of my life, as I am still constantly working through them myself. But then I asked myself, "What if there is someone out there who needs to hear your story? Can you really forgive yourself if you give up on the opportunity to impact someone else's life?"

As you already know I could not forgive myself if I had passed this opportunity by. I know for a fact that there are so many others with similar stories that are still suffering and struggling and think that they are alone. I'm here to tell you that you are not alone, you are not the only one who has gone through something like this and you do NOT have to be a victim. You are beautifully and wonderfully made, so start owning it and stop being complacent with where you are right now. Strive for more because you deserve more. We are all broken in this world, but it is those who are broken that make the most impact. Don't be afraid to tell your story and share what you have learned so far. I know that it's hard and that at times you don't see the light on the other side, but you need to actively reach and search for that light to find it. And then you need to go out and become that light for someone else. No matter what you have experienced in life thus far, know that it is all for a reason. I know that the things I experienced have made me stronger and more confident in myself. It has also given me the opportunity to impact the lives of others that are still in that dark place. Don't give up!

About Samantha Parma-Vera

Samantha is a student of Florida Atlantic University and is currently pursuing her degrees the field of Psychology. She is the Global Ambassador for Youth Victim Services for Elite Foundation. Samantha has been devoted to the Foundation from its inception; and has been a voice of advocacy for the voiceless thousands entrapped in modern day enslavement. But her personal story began when she was a teenager. Samantha's story as a naïve 15-year-old girl, lost and unsure of who she is becoming, is not unlike all of us. However, she was caught in and up in the social lies of a deviant sexual subculture that plagues are children today.

Her story is unique, and she is ready to share it with the YOU. As you read her chapter, you will be taken into the darker parts of her past and follow her journey from being a victim to becoming a victor over her demons. Against insidious evil, she pulls through and now she has a message to share and a passion to help those in her generation and beyond, who are struggling with becoming VICTORS.

CHAPTER 9

BBQ

By: Kenda Peterson

One of my earliest recollections of my childhood is of playing hide and seek with family and friends in our old home. A pre-teen/teenage boy told me to hide in the closet with him. Something inside of me did not want to walk into that closet that day; however, I did. I went into the dark closet against my inner voice, and out of it emerged from that darkness a different child.

From that moment, most of my life has been a series of internal struggles, for there in a closet, in an old home, my life forever changed. The heart of a young, carefree child, the ability to play and be me with reckless abandonment died and out of that death a child became shattered; my soul would be forever changed. Thus, began the tapestry of my life, some bright and beautiful, some torn and worn thin, all shape the woman I am today.

Join me as we look back on us. For somewhere in the lines of these pages lies words you need, as much as I do. I need you, you need me. We were not meant to carry the load alone, we were not meant to have many of the things that have happened to us, happen, but they did; and together, let's shed light on it. Together we will no longer remain that shattered little girl, but the powerful warrior we were designed to be!

Let's begin, and we will begin where we are, in the here and now, going back to see that which we are supposed to discover, together. Before we do, let's promise to be true to who we are no matter how painful and ugly it may be!

Things aren't always as they appear on the outside, take me for example. Right now, I am sitting in my place after having one of the most emotionally painful seasons of my life; friends (new and old), coworkers, business associates strangers and I meet, look and see me. Many are in awe of me, that I left what was comfortable to step out and begin something in a "foreign land", or a land that is foreign to me, that is.

Even while in the grip of God Himself, all of us are vulnerable to becoming prey to a predator, especially those of us who have already been targeted, it is as if we send out signals to those whom are not trustworthy, it happens throughout our lives, it seems it never stops.

Why do I always attract those that will harm me?

Are we "labeled" do those whom have it out to harm others that innately, acutely aware?

Or am I just plain nuts?

Tell me you haven't asked yourself those same questions, we who have been hurt can't help it because we know it is not the grand design of how things are to be, especially when it began when you were so young.

The childhood recollection was of a girl at a very young age, and now over 35 years later, I became prey once again. Recently in fact. My predator, was not hiding in the closet this time, no, he disguised himself in his profession, licensed therapist, preying on me in my most vulnerable state. Once again, I walked into the setting, as if it were the same house with the closet of my childhood trauma, and once again I emerged wronged. A man who made a professional vow to help others, went against it. I'm still grappling with the thought, "Was it to intentionally hurt me? To feed his ego rather than help me?" I do not know, I may never know, because like those that have gone before him he chose not to take ownership or responsibility but chose to belittle, tear down, lie and try to destroy me.

This time however, I am pissed! Finally, enough is enough. So, together, you and I, we are going to help one another so this never happens again, not to us and hopefully not to another.

Anyone who has been the product of some form of abuse realizes what that does to a person's psyche. Each day in a survivor's life may include constant battles for the mind, heart and soul...each day a battle for my mind and soul begins, some days within the deepest parts of me is vision, purpose, compassion, inner-strength, passion, forgiveness, trust in God, tenderness toward others, loved, victor, strong, daring, willful, chosen. Then in a millisecond I would have thoughts like you're too passive, unworthy, worthless, weak, Co-dependent, destined to be alone, self-doubt, disappointment, self-sabotage, anger at God and self, ugly, fat, broken use, the list can go on and on. I realize now that most of all I am down right scared!

I am an analyzer...I think things to death, to the point of utter paralysis at times. I honestly think it stems as deep down as to the little girl who went against her tender heart, she thought, "this doesn't feel right to go in there", but she went, and now she doubts all her emotions, even who she is at times.

I sit here angry, alone, in need of finances and fearful of the next step I am to take, but I have sat still too long it is time to fight! I am fighting for the little girl who went into the closet, the young girl who had to grow up too fast, the teen who was too serious to fully live, the twenty-something me who became guarded, the thirty-something me who wandered a different path only to harm herself more and now for all of us!

It took a therapist with his professional degree to hurt me in such an unethical way, a way I as a protector of others cannot understand or accept. This is where I draw the line! This is where I fight! The sweet, kind, knows what to say to others, she just decided to become head bitch. I am not talking in a vulgar sense of the word, but the use of the words is to identify the word "boundaries", because up until this point in my life, a nice woman never fought back....and it is time to fight!

I mentioned my fears...I am fearful, but can no longer stay silent, anger rushes through my veins to make sense of my life. God, dear God, why?! Why me?! Why didn't YOU stop it, why haven't YOU protected me?! Why?!!! WHY?! I yell, and I scream, and I ask God over and repeatedly, and nothing changes. Or does it? Out of the shadows of my anger, my questions, my tears... after all my self-sufficiency and energy are depleted I breathe and that same part of my soul that was there that day that when I was little and so many other days, in the stillness of my questions, doubts, hurts, anger, victories and flat out numbness there she is, TRUTH....

Although she was taught "vengeance is God's" she realized, somewhere deep within her is a mighty warrior...she was Viking Princess, all her life her daddy told her that, for that was why she was given that name, and it was time to fight....to fight for the soul that was robbed to fight for all those carrying the same burden, to fight for those who are after her, just now being preyed upon and to fight to stop others from having to go down those same twists and turns. It was time for her to fight against all odds!

She is on her own. Money is gone, no family, friends or man nearby, nothing to distract or numb the pain, all she has is herself and the power within her, is that enough? She wonders, "Do I have power?"

Some people think that there is no such thing as evil, there is. Sometimes evil is an outward force trying to hurt the innocence of youth, sometimes evil is in the acts of grown people who have their own agenda, who either want to harm you, or keep you in a box for their sake. Sometimes evil is envy and sometimes evil is the lies we tell ourselves as we allow those feelings we have within our souls to destroy the very being of who we are created to be!

All, yes, every one of those evils have been done to me and to be honest there have been times I am guilty of such to others, but the evil that hurts me the most right now, is the evil I have done to myself.

Remember our vow. We will go on this journey together, no matter how ugly? Here is where the journey lies, it is the beginning and we are amid the labyrinth...

Emotions are my biggest obstacle to overcome because they are real, and I have gone against the healthy ones for so long, so I feed them, love them and nurture the ones that are lies. Why do I love to do that? They become all-consuming they are hard for me to overcome. I can blame it on the abuse, or because as a Generation X'er I was taught to be seen not heard, no time to discuss much as a matter of fact, we were told to keep it secret.

Second obstacle is to fight for myself, I can fight for truth for others and I am fantastic at fighting for causes, but for me? Unheard of until now...that girl was lead into a closet of an old home years ago, and the woman I am. Can the warrior within me rise? Yes, she can. Yes, she is. And she will continue to.

We must stick together we whom have overcome, we have blindly felt our way through this labyrinth of life, we have tripped and lost our way at times, yet we have survived. We have not been defeated; we are able to withstand some of the most horrific things. I have chosen not to disclose all I have been through, maybe one day I will, I promise you it is more than I should have ever been through, as I am sure so is your pain.

They only loss, is when we allow the thoughts that are lies to take root in our heart, in our mind and in our soul. Then those whom tried to destroy us win. We must find others who we can walk through this life with us, people who can tell us the truth, and the truth is you are conqueror, that every good and perfect thought is truth, we must defeat that which wants to harm us, truth...no more lies, we after all deserve to be all we were designed to be.

I have been abused in so many forms, I have had to carry a child within my womb after one of those instances, only for me never to carry a child within me again, but none of those define who I am. I am who I am because of these experiences.

Every single hurt and pain that I have exposed to others has been used for good. They have made me hard on myself, I have caused pain to me, but they have also helped me to be kind, compassionate, fighter of souls, understanding, tender, vulnerable, able to love, feel and fight.

Life hasn't turned out the way I planned, but it is beautiful none the less, someone once told me "It is all those cracks in your life Kenda that allow all the light to shine through." At times do I wish I was not cracked, sure but most days I see I really am stronger than I think, and so are you!

I leave you with the words to a song, "BBQ" by ALO (Animal Liberation Orchestra)

The road is long and windy like a good mystery unfolding

It twists and turns in colorful subplots and sunburns and fake out endings.

And sometimes my patience in the whole process starts bending.

As I attempt to unravel the web by traversing and rehearsing and persevering along the doubt-laden extension cord thread of my life.

And in this life we're free to dream whatever we want to, but that doesn't mean that your dreams are gonna to come true

Instead as a way of getting us to move

Life dangles your dreams in front of you

And unable to resist the temptation, we continue

And it's clear to me that this life is gonna be

All about the dangling possibilities that keep turning in and turning out

Yes it's clear to me that this life is gonna be

All about the dangling possibilities

The road is long and windy

Full of twists and turns

But before you can rise from the ashes

You've got to burn baby burn

Welcome to your barbeque

Where we roast all the dreams

That never came true

Welcome to your barbeque

Pig out and dream a new

So, the therapist? We will see what happens with that. Police are involved, and I am in for the fight of my life...a fight like I have never had before, and I fight that before now I was afraid to step into. But not anymore! I realized on Thanksgiving night when my nephews and family were with me, I have an obligation to the next generation. I am armed with TRUTH, I am ready to FIGHT, I am not taking this laying down...for now, welcome to my barbeque where I roast all the dreams that never came true. Welcome to my barbeque, let's pig out and dream anew!

And, sometime soon I hope the nightmare with the evil therapist will have a solid, happy ending but even if it shouldn't. It won't matter, because I am invincible!

"Forgiveness means giving up all hope of a better past."

About Kenda Peterson

Kenda Peterson has spent over 20 years working with youth to equip and empower them with life skills.

Kenda has dedicated her life to helping the next generation know they have a voice, they are able to overcome, as well as help them to discover their true identity. Kenda currently resides in Jacksonville, Florida where she has the honor of leading a team of indigenous missionaries who mentor teens in the Duval, Clay, St Johns and Nassau counties.

CHAPTER 10

HOW TO BECOME

By: Stacey Garlin Lederberg

The very first time I thought to write a book was a few months after I had been binge/purge free for 1 year. It had been 11 years of hating myself, my body and at the one-year mark, I wanted to share my story and an idea was born. The title I had dreamed of was, "How to Become." I never truly knew how to explain the title, but throughout my life I have been searching for my truth. I have been figuring out who I was to become, so the title just seemed to fit. I was never quite sure how to become me. At that time, I didn't have an answer to that question, but with some in depth work on me and my life, I believe I have learned how to become me!

I often think a lot about where I have been geographically and metaphorically. I reflect on the process that it took to get to where I am now. Thich Nhat Hanh, the Vietnamese Zen Buddhist spiritual leader, says, "No mud, no lotus." Without suffering through the mud, you cannot find the happiness of the lotus. According to this wise man, the secret to happiness is to acknowledge and transform suffering, not to run away from it. In order for the beauty of the lotus to shine one petal at a time, it first must sit in the muck and mud of the waters. While the muck is not pleasant, it is essential for the growth of the flower. While I don't believe I am done growing and learning, I have learned the hard way how to love my body in whatever form it is. I have learned to love who I am from the inside out. It has not been an easy road, and I have sat in the mud for weeks, months, and sometimes years, but I am here, I am amazing, and I am loved!

My story begins in childhood, and for all intents and purposes, mine was great. It was mostly free from drama and hardships. However, it wasn't always easy. I grew up in a typical household at the time, with a mother and a father living together. I had a mother, who was demanding and critical of every aspect of my life, and father who doted on his youngest child (me), one sibling and a cat, at least for a short period of time. We had a nice life. My father was a hard worker and up until I entered middle school my mother was a stay at home mom. I was a happy kid, with many friends, and was active. In high school, I was a cheerleader, which carries with it a set of rules sometimes hard to live up to.

I graduated from high school and attended a college within the acceptable distance from home. At college I learned how to be me, without the day to day influence of my mother. While I wasn't exactly fat, I wasn't exactly skinny and during my college career, played several Varsity sports. As an athlete, I was obsessive about my body and my weight but joining crew and rowing in a lightweight boat was the most devastating to my overall self-esteem. I had been put on a lightweight team as a "boat maker", because I was smaller than most of the girls on the team. What that means is I was there to ensure that the boat average weight did not go over 125. I was 5'6", had less than 20% body fat and was made to get down to 115 lbs. That was the start of many of my weight and body image issues. It became a roller coaster of up and down, guilt when I wasn't making weight and elation when I was. That was my life, up and down, heavy and light. At that time, my life was like a car that was stuck in the mud. Constantly spinning my wheels, leaving little energy to get out. Thankfully after 2 years of lightweight crew, it was over and I no longer had that pressure from my coach, but only from me as I still was obsessed with being the perfect "looking" athlete. I maintained my cover of disordered eating because truthfully no one was looking.

Once out of college, in the working world of teaching and living in NYC, I was slowly losing my collegiate athlete's body. My days of over exercising were over, and the weight just kept creeping on. That was when the cycle of anorexia and bulimia began. I weighed as little as 105 lbs. and as much as 175 and everything in between for 11 years. I was trudging through the quicksand that was constantly pulling me down, and it was difficult to break the cycle. Moving along with a heaviness that felt like I would never get out. It wasn't until I woke up one day in bed, lying in blood, and knew there had to be a better way. I drove myself to the hospital and when I got there, thinking there was something truly wrong, I was completely embarrassed when I was told by the doctors, "it was just my period". And that was the first time I thought, this madness has got to stop. And for the very first time of many, I began to turn my life around. I pulled myself out of the mud and began the process of healing.

My story, however, is much more than my wonderful childhood and the start of my addiction. In my 5 decades of life, I have been diagnosed with an anxiety disorder, depression, bulimia, anorexia and other forms of eating disorders. I have had weight issues my entire life, I was too skinny or too fat but never just right. I suffered from poor body image, low self-esteem and never quite felt accepted for who I was. Even with my best friends, I never felt like I belonged. I was always searching for the perfect me and never felt quite enough.

I left teaching and went back to graduate school for counseling. During this time is when I truly solidified my recovery from the eating disorders that plagued me for, so long. I graduated with my second master's degree and I was no more than I was before, except now there was more debt. While learning how to counsel others, I fell in love with someone whom I thought was my forever, got my heart crushed, and knocked a few more pegs off my self-esteem. In my life, I had never had a romantic relationship that was healthy, or good. They always seemed to be sitting in the mud at the bottom of the pond and that I struggled in this area, more than most. I would get involved with men who were just not right for me, but thought they were. Because I believed at the time this was my forever person and I was proved wrong, it just solidified my thought that I was not good enough. I now had 2 master's degrees and was still unsure of who I was, and was floundering in a sea of mud, self-doubt and insecurity.

The famous mindfulness guru, Jon Kabat-Zinn writes, "wherever you go, there you are". And for me that couldn't be truer.

While I had moved to several states, changed jobs, met and kept a significant pond of friends, my issues of low self-esteem and poor body image, moved with me. I was trying to find my way and always bringing my issues with me. I still felt lost all the time. I was counseling others and, felt like a fraud. I was teaching adolescent girls about how to get out from their mud which consisted of low self-esteem and poor body image, and I was suffering from both. While I could help others in the classroom and in therapy, I could not help myself. My life continued to be a mess, where I had brief periods of being that lotus and then quickly getting stuck back in the mud. Depression and anxiety were present off and on and the therapists I saw just piled on more and different meds to help me, but they never quite did.

And then in one instance, my life took a major turn, I got a serious blow that kept me down so far in the mud, it would take years before I would get out. A week before I was moving to Florida to spend more time with my aging parents, my mother died. It was the last week of school before I was moving, a Monday when I got a call that will reverberate in my head forever.

I picked up the phone and it was my father on the other end, and all he said was "mommy's dead". I screamed so loud that my coworkers came running. The rest of the day was a blur, but somehow people had helped me get to the airport and down to Florida for a funeral.

My mother and I had a somewhat difficult relationship. While deep down I knew I was loved immensely by her, I never felt it was without conditions. I loved my mother deeply and spoke to her nearly every day, but when she was taken from me, suddenly and without notice it changed the course of my life. I never got to say goodbye, and never got to tell her I loved her one last time. My last ever thought about my mother while she was still alive, was this:

Seeing her name on my caller ID that Sunday evening, I said "ah, I don't feel like talking to her now, I will call her tomorrow".

Tomorrow never came, as she passed in her sleep. I still moved to Florida, but now it was to "take care" of my Dad, who was so overwhelmed with grief he was barely functioning. So instead of starting a new life in Florida, I was moving in with my Dad. That was nearly 12 years ago.

I learned many things from my mother. Not all of what was learned was good or healthy. She had an unhealthy obsession with her body, my body and with getting me married. It was always a huge part of every conversation I ever had with her. "How much do you weigh now, and when are you getting married?" I am pretty sure it didn't happen like that, however, it seemed that way to me. She was always commenting on my lack of makeup, my messy hair, my body and my clothing choices. I never felt like I was living up to her expectations. I still remember one day listening to her speak with a friend about me. I don't think she knew I could hear her, but she was telling her friend that I was going to travel in Europe for 6 weeks, by myself only taking 1 backpack. Her reaction of me, to her friend was, "I can't believe she's my daughter, if I wasn't there when she was born, I might not believe she were mine." Even though I knew she didn't mean that, it has stuck with me deeply. But the truth is, my story isn't about how my mother treated me or didn't treat me. As I always tried to get others to see, it is never about what other people think, it took me a long time to fully embrace that myself. I knew that I had to reframe her constant criticisms, but it took me a forever to get there.

And then I had a daughter. She didn't come easy. I met a man, who I truly thought I was in love with, but at a time in which I was still grieving the sudden loss of my mother. In the first year after my mother passed, I was very dissociated from the Stacey I had always known. I had no energy, I cared about very little and was going through the motions of living life daily. When I met my now ex-husband, I was someone who, I did not recognize. But nonetheless, we met, and within 9 months we were married. Fifteen months later through IVF, our daughter was born. The day I found out that I was having a girl, I got a call from the nurse as I had just had some genetic testing, and she said, "You are having a beautiful healthy baby girl." I couldn't believe my ears, healthy AND a girl. I asked my then husband to please call the nurse back to make sure I heard her correctly. At that moment, panic set in. I am having a girl. I am surely going to f**@ her up. I was 44 at the time of my daughter's birth. It took me a long time to be a mom! And the day she was bo rn, was the happiest day of my entire life. The moment she was put in my arms, I thanked my mother for making it happen. For being that source of comfort knowing all along that she was watching over me, protecting us, and ensuring her granddaughter's birth.

Pregnancy however was very hard on me. To someone with a history of eating disorders, gaining that much weight was overwhelmingly difficult. At one point near the end of my pregnancy I asked the doctor to not tell me, my current weight. I just couldn't handle the thought of being close to 200 pounds. My baby girl was a large baby, so I gained an enormous amount of weight. Early in my pregnancy, I didn't want to leave the house, because I didn't really look pregnant, I just looked fat and I didn't want to be judged. Shortly into my second trimester someone finally asked me when I was due, and I was thrilled because I finally looked pregnant. It was only then I truly felt comfortable going out of the house.

So here I was, a 44-year-old first time mother and all I could do was stare at her, because I couldn't believe she was mine. Every day I prayed for the strength to be a good mother, a kind mother and a loving mother who was like the beautiful lotus. A symbol of rebirth and strength. I didn't want to instill the wrong ideas in her, and my biggest fear is that she too would develop an eating disorder, have anxiety or depression. Her father too had health issues, and weight issues ran in both of our families. This causes me a great deal of worry. I knew I had to do better, as I knew I had to change my thoughts, my feelings and my overall attitude about myself and my body. I knew I had to be the kind of role model that I wanted for my daughter.

But overcoming 25+ years of negativity about oneself is certainly not easy. I was so immersed in raising that little girl, working hard and finding me, that it left little time for much else, including my marriage.

And then one morning it happened. I woke up and realized I was overwhelmingly unhappy. I had become someone I did not know. I was married to a man with whom I had so little in common with, we agreed on nothing. And I knew that I had to do better for myself and my daughter. I told my husband I wanted out. He was not the man I wanted to live with for the rest of my life. His ideas and values were so differentfrom mine that I didn't see any way to agree. I didn't want counseling, I couldn't save the marriage, I wanted out and I wanted me back. I wanted to be Stacey again, whatever that meant. I wanted to find me. But we had a 4-year-old and it broke my heart to know that her life changed that very day. We stayed together 3 more years after that day, as I wanted to try and stay for the sake of my daughter. But one day the ex-woke up, believed he had the hope of a new girlfriend and decided it was time to get a divorce. Just like the speedy marriage, there was a speedy divorce. Within 3 months he moved out and within another 5 months it was done.

I will never forget the day, June 25, 2016. The last of the ex's stuff was taken from the house. He had decided, without any input from me, it was good for our daughter to spend the first night in his new place with him. I was alone. I was sad. I was happy. I was free. I felt as if a black cloud had been blown away from above my head. I felt light. Then I started the process of cleansing and reclaiming me. I got out my sage and smudged the entire house. I prayed for the strength to live life on my terms. I then began the process of cleansing my living space. And when I was done, I breathed for the first time in years. I called a friend, she brought over a pizza, and kept me smiling all the while I felt a heaviness in my heart from the absence of my baby. In her lifetime, up to that point I had only spend a handful of days away from her. I couldn't believe that now, 30% of her time would be spent without me. When my friend left I sat on the beach chair I was now using as a couch and cried. I cried for me. I cried for my baby.

But mostly I cried out of sheer joy at the lightness I felt. At that moment, I knew that I had done the right thing. I wanted my daughter to know that her parent's relationship was not the norm, and that she deserved to be in a mutually loving, unconditional amazing relationship.

And so, did I!

I have come to understand a great deal about myself over the past 18 months. I have an insatiable desire to learn. I want a healthy, well balanced life in mind, body and spirit. I have studied positive psychology, researched about happiness, and I have read extensively about Buddhism. I am contemplative, and I never stop seeking ways to increase my mental, physical and spiritual self. I am connected deeply with my God and truly believe that all the while, when things were falling apart, he was putting them into the right place for me. Staying positive when your world is crumbling around you is no easy task. Yet, in the end, I like to imagine that every negative and positive thing that has happened, has been there to help me to turn my life around. I believe much of what has happened over the course of my life has been my given path. While I don't mean that free will didn't play a part in my decisions, I know much of what transpired was God's way of telling me, I wasn't done figuring it all out. I believe that a lesson is repeated until it is learned, and I had many lessons to learn and even repeated some of them, until they were learned. Sometimes it seemed unfair, but I have a multitude of blessings that I am thankful for every day. I know that life is neither fair or unfair; it simply is whatever it happens to be. That is one of the greatest lessons I have learned.

I then began the process of figuring out how to heal my body and my mind. My body came first as I was feeling horrible, I was overweight, my biometric numbers were not good, and I woke up each morning with so much pain in my body that I couldn't walk. I was stuck at the bottom of the pond and I needed a way out. I knew there had to be a connection to what I was eating and how my body felt. After an extensive amount of research, seeing many different doctors, I did the only thing I could do, I tried an elimination diet. I eliminated all inflammatory foods, sugar, gluten (and all grains), legumes, soy, and dairy. Then what happened was short of a miracle. After a few short days, my body began the healing process. I woke up with less and less pain as the days went by. I knew I was onto something and I continued for a full 30 days. My mind was clearer, my body was feeling great and I was so excited to wake up every morning with no pain. It was the first time in almost 6 years. It was then I realized I have the power to heal my body with what I put in my body.

While my body was feeling great and my mind was clearing, I was missing a spiritual connection. It was during that time, I reconnected with a past love, the one who I believed was my forever. He was always a strong spiritual presence in my life and he was there for me at a time when I was struggling with leaving my husband. After my divorce, we met up one weekend and after 20 years of friendship had a whirlwind romance for six months and then just like that he disappeared again. I learned at that moment, I finally learned, I am worth much more than being with someone who cannot be there for me. That lesson has repeated itself many times in my life. This time it was much less devastating then the last time. I was stronger. I was surer of myself and realized that it was him and not me. This was an important lesson to learn. I am worth it!

As my body healed, my mind followed, and it became much clearer that what I needed to heal was my past. It was the day I walked into a Mindful Based Stress Reduction class. My anxiety high and I knew that meditation had the potential to reduce that stress. Learning mindfulness created an entire new path for my daughter and me. I know that meditation has the power to heal and try to meditate daily with her. Of course, we don't always succeed, and that is ok. To my daughter, I like to call us perfectly imperfect or as my daughter says, "imperfectly perfect". Some days we succeed and some days we fail, either way, we are OK.

My body was healing, my mind and spirituality were healing and that left me with what I wanted to do with the rest of my life. While teaching will always be my passion, I know that I want more.

While trying to sort through the issues with my body and my food, my daughter was having her own issues. Finding the right combination of foods for her as well, has been a process, but through that process I became interested in helping others that also have these issues. I began coursework at the Institute for Integrative Nutrition to become a health and wellness coach. I love knowing our bodies have the unlimited potential to tell us exactly what we need and what we don't need.

My body was clearly telling me what I could no longer eat, and my daughter's body was doing the same. It is a process, but I'm confident in our food choices these days. Some days we get off track, but sometimes a girl just needs a good slice of pizza. Thankfully now, I can eat the pizza happily with my daughter and with joy, move on and we then go back to our gluten free, dairy free and sugar free life. Perfectly imperfect is the way we go through life these days and it feels good. It's too much pressure to be perfect, and that pressure can just push you down in the monotony of the mud.

I feel blessed to have had these experiences and lessons that have led me to where I am now. When I think about who I am, I must laugh, because just weeks ago when my daughter was overwhelmed with stress about her upcoming cheer competition, I played "I am woman" by Helen Reddy. I think she thought I was crazy at the time, because in her words "this is such an old song mama" but when she got out on the mat, popping in her head was...I am strong, I am invincible, I am woman! That is how I feel. While I am not perfect, I am perfectly imperfect in every way. Perfectly imperfect in my dealings with my daughter, with my students, with my clients, with my family and friends, my ex-husband and with myself. I am on a path to heal my mind, my soul and most importantly my body. I have been tough on my body through the course of my life and it's tired and sometimes uncooperative. But I have come through it all with a new-found freedom from food. No longer does food or my weight have a hold on me. As Popeye says, "I am, what I am" and I am lovable, kind, generous, smart and caring, and want to use all of that in the service of others. To help others see that they too are perfectly imperfect and that is OK. I am very much like the lotus flower! I went through and sat in the mud and muck and I have come out on top a beautiful flower, admired by all who see it.

About Stacey Lederberg

Stacey is an educator and counselor with over 20 years' experience teaching and helping others. She has taught in New York City at the School for the Deaf, in Atlanta, Georgia and now in Boca Raton, Florida. Her career has included teaching children with special needs including those with autism, counseling adolescent addicts and adolescent girls with eating disorders.

Stacey was instrumental in the creation of the primary program for the Body and Soul National Institute which served to help adolescent girls overcome poor self-esteem and body image. She worked as a partner in The Bigger Half, which primarily assisted corporations with leadership and speaking skills. Along the way Stacey also found the time to utilize her love of the outdoors to teach teens how to overcome obstacles using experiential education and outdoor ropes courses.

Stacey is a daughter, sister, aunt, friend, and teacher and has struggled, with depression, anxiety, bulimia, and anorexia. And currently is living in the aftermath of a divorce and with the struggle of being a single mother. These struggles have proven her strength and determination in overcoming hardships and learning how to live a gratefully blessed life.

Stacey has a master's Degree in Counseling and Special Education and a bachelor's in Health and Wellness. Now after 3 decades of schooling and working, she is joining all her past experiences to be a Health/Life Coach. Stacey is earning a certificate at the Institute for Integrative Nutrition in Holistic Health and Nutrition in which she is learning over 100 dietary theories as well as preventive medicine, and the balance of physical, mental and spiritual health. Her focus is to help families, especially mothers, overcome the stress of parenting, working and learning how to live a healthy life. She has been certified in Mindful Based Stress Reduction (MBSR) and will utilize that knowledge in combination with her education to promote a mindful life. Stacey's company Mindful Holistic Health with work with clients to enhance one's health and learn how to live stress-free through nutrition, lifestyle management and mindful living. Visit her at:

www.mindfulholistichealth.com.

CHAPTER 11

IF WALLS COULD TALK

By: Marquita Williams

"There is not one experience, no matter how devastating, no matter how torturous it may appear to have been, there is nothing ever wasted. Everything that is happening to you is being drawn into your life as a means to help you evolve into who you were really meant to be here on Earth. It's not the thing that matters, it's what that thing opens within you. "

- Oprah

Everyone has a story. My hope is that my personal truth, the one that I share with you, resonates in some way, demonstrates triumph that you might identify with, and provides a tool that you might use to stand in your own shame with confidence and find the momentum to look up from the point of where you are now and give birth to laser focus on where you're going. I'll share with you a compilation of tragedies, however in it lives a message around mercy, grace, persistence, and the willingness to survive.

I grew up in the projects in a mid-size apartment unit complex. Our two-bedroom apartment was maybe 600 square feet, and I shared a bedroom with my two brothers. That apartment was a representation of hell to me. My mother was a functioning alcoholic and was addicted to prescription drugs. She was always angry, and it was obvious something that happened in her life caused her to suffer and have much pain. Almost every night, she followed the same brutal routine, the stereo turned on around 9:00 pm every night, she poured herself a glass of Tanqueray, once intoxicated she'd walk around the house cursing me. The music would play until the early hours of the morning. I'm not exactly sure why, but most of her anger was towards me, as I cannot remember her deflecting any of her pain on my two brothers, and because of it, I experienced a significant amount of emotional, mental, and physical abuse for many years.

She was not a loving mother. She was not affectionate, nor told me she loved me, and I cannot ever remember a time when I felt love for her. She would always yell at me, I could never do anything right, and physical beatings were routine. If I didn't bring the television remote fast enough, she beat me. If I was tasked with food shopping and didn't buy all the right groceries, she would beat me. She always found a reason to beat me. Many of my adolescent years were spent doing adult things. By the age of 10, I could cook, wash our weekly laundry, as well as shop for groceries, clothes, and personal shopping. Most of the horrible things I was exposed to, was right there, in front of me, in my own home. I witnessed drug use, drug sales, and domestic abuse was the norm, every man my mother had a relationship with beat her. Usually after a night of booze, domestic arguments would quickly escalate. Those nights were so long. Hours and hours of yelling, cursing, and the sounds of furniture being tossed around the house kept me awake most nights. I'd peek out of my bedroom door, just to see my mother dragged across the floor, objects thrown at her petite body, as she lay on the ground, while at the same time trying her best to escape as many punches as possible. Her head knocked up against the wall, lamps picked up and tossed at her face and the next morning, love was demonstrated to me as seeing that same man wake up, cook breakfast, and watch the Sunday football game with us as, if nothing had happened. I'm unable to delicately describe the pain that I felt in that space and time, and I could go on about what I did not learn during this young age, but I'll focus on what I did learn.

I am Strong.

I learned survivorship and how to provide for myself and get through each day. Life was depressing, but I cannot remember a time where it took an exclusive hold on my heart. I always had this confidence and remained hopeful that one day I would get out of this hell and never look back. My birth mother died when I was 26 years old. A few weeks before she died, she requested my brothers and I to visit her in the hospital, where she was receiving hospice palliative care. During our visit, my body was present in the room, but I was emotionless, and felt no pain knowing I'd never see her again.

Today, I hold no judgement of my mother. Even imperfect she made a difference in my life. God knew he was going to bless me with children in a big way, and for me to navigate through that new and exciting journey, he would need to equip me with unmeasurable strength to love my children unconditionally, even in the presence of masked pain and suffering.

I am Joyous.

My biological paternal grandparents helped me to find the strength I needed to get through my childhood pain. Like many black children raised in poverty, my grandparents mostly raised me during the early years of my childhood. They loved me unconditionally and provided love and safe shelter. Even if perhaps their initial desire to help raise me stemmed from the passing of their son, my father. My birth father died when he was 23, when I was just three years old, from Non-Hodgins Lymphoma. I'm always saddened when I hear someone describe moments or memories of happiness from their childhood with their dads, as I do not have those memories. There is one memory that I remember vividly. On this occasion, my grandparents dressed me in a white long sleeve ruffled shirt that tucked into blue pleated skirt. I wore white stockings with black dress shoes. My hair was in ponytails. I remember feeling very pretty. Riding in a stretch limousine, we arrived at a church, where I sat in the first pew. When I looked up, I remember seeing a shiny brown coffin with my father lying in it. At three years old, I was attending my father's funeral.

I'd give anything to have other memories of my father. His funeral, is the one and only memory that I have of him. I'm sure the passing of my father was tough on my grandparents, and equally as challenging to take on the responsibility of having to help raise me. My grandfather did his best to fill this void, he was so good to me and loved me very much. His care and protection will forever remain in my heart.

I am Grateful.

At an early age, my grandparents and aunts encouraged me to read books that matched my interest, instantly I developed a love for reading, and read every book I could get my hands on. Reading became an outlet for me to discover what the outside world beyond an apartment could be like. Sweet Valley High, Nancy Drew, and Goosebumps series were a few of my favorites, immersed in every word, I'd morph into the characters. Their adventures became my adventures. They became my mentors, friends, confidants, and most importantly my escape.

I am Extraordinary.

When I was 12 years old, I met an angel and one of the kindest souls walking this Earth. Initially, just trying to make a difference, she volunteered her time and mentored a few of the girls at our school. Enrolled in a program created for high risk students, she was introduced to me as someone that I could hang out with and call my big sister, my cousin and I developed a one on one relationship with her, fast forward a few years, I was blessed with the opportunity to just call her "Mom". For the first time in my life, I had a mother figure who expressed love and cared for me. Authentically, **she loved me**, she paid attention to me, and committed to the little things that made a difference like helping me with my homework, and school assignments. Eating in a restaurant and shopping for clothes in a shopping mall were overwhelming experiences but, it was the best feeling in the world to me. I'd pick up the cutest clothes with matching jewelry and hair ties. What was this strong emotion I was feeling? It was love, and her ability to effortlessly begin to change my life made it easier to breathe and gave me hope and excitement about renewed life.

My mom constantly talked with me about life, how the world works, and shared with me important life lessons. She made sure that I was aware that all things are possible, and was possible for me. Because we were different races, we talked about all things black and white, and did her best to help me to navigate race related challenges that I'd most certainly experience. Unfortunately, these experiences gave birth to rejection. A few of my friends teased me for being "too white", and on the other hand, the white kids at school didn't want to hang out with me and teased me for being "too ghetto." **I didn't fit in anywhere.** Although these were tough conversations for us, my mom would never simply say it would be ok or urge me to get over these experiences, she helped me to accept my thoughts and feelings and work through them. She was so good at explaining everything.

I am Blessed.

If I had not grown up with adversities and experienced abusive pain, I most likely would have never met my mom. My life could have gone so differently, so it is evident to me now that those tragedies and God's grace blessed me with a mom that would authentically provide true happiness. Of all the lessons she's taught me, forgiveness is the most impactful. It was not until she delicately explained to me what illness looks like and the various reasons for my birth mother's abuse, that I began the healing process to forgive her for all the pain she had caused me.

I am Happy.

I've always had a desire to become a teacher. When I was in elementary school, I would ask my friends to play school with me. We would meet in an open field near the complex playground, and I'd ask them to pretend like we were in a classroom. We would pretend school for hours. I was the teacher, assigned homework and helped all my "students" with classroom work. One day I remembered seeing teacher aides throw away paper assignments and workbooks in the garbage, so I decided to walk over to our Elementary School and take them out of the school dumpster, so we could have textbooks and actual paper assignments to use for the homework assignments. Funny thing, without the validation from my birth mom, I just knew school grades were important and my early adolescent "career" in teaching would somehow pay off. This playtime played a significant role in who I am today.

At 16, I graduated the top of my class in high school, and immediately after graduation, I enrolled in courses at the local community college, after a bit I quickly became bored with my plan to obtain an Accounting/Marketing degree and began contemplating dropping out of college. That was until I saw an open house advertisement for an ultrasound program in the local newspaper. I know now more than ever that was no coincidence and someone had other plans for me. Plans to prosper me, not to harm me, and give me a future. (Jeremiah 29:11) I did not drop out, and instead graduated with honors from the Sonography program, Sonography has opened many doors for me and paved the way to many leadership opportunities. For the past 7 years, I've enjoyed serving the ultrasound community, as a college professor, and now I have the opportunity to help others, empower them to see their dreams come true and encourage them to keep going no matter how tough it is. Taking textbooks and practice exams out the school dumpster wasn't a bad idea after all. I see it as my first job interview and I passed talent review with flying colors.

I am Abundant.

When I was 13 years old, the summer before 9th grade, I met my high school sweetheart. He was one of the popular kids at school, and although I was not, we had an immediate connection to each other and instantly began a friendship. We talked every day on the phone. Hung out with one another at and after school. He was my best friend and soon I became his. He was an amazing guy, and in just one year, he was not just the love of my life but also the father of my first son. Again, the feelings of hard luck resurfaced and for the first time, I became very disappointed in myself for making such a big mistake, and scared sick of what everyone would think of me. I was 14 and pregnant. We dealt with the shame for a few months, but very quickly worked together to keep each other focused solely on graduating high school and taking care of our son. And we did just that.

We supported each other through our mess, we talked about our future often and planned each step of our lives together.

I've spent twenty-five amazing years of my life with him. We married in 2004 and honor one another the same as we did that summer before 9th grade. What a blessing to move through my life with my high school crush, who became my boyfriend, who became my babys daddy, who became my fiancé, and later my husband and the love of my life. We are in love and still are happily married.

If you are determined to be successful, teenage pregnancy does not have to be the end of your story. Motherhood began for me at the age of 14, and although I was very young, life experiences prepared me for an early transition into motherhood. Quickly I began to understand how each of those experiences will play apart in my ability to demonstrate I could be a loving parent, loving wife, loving daughter, and commit to self-love.

I am Obedient.

I've had so many impediments in my life, but God has remained faithful to his word to keep me. I've always listened to my mother's advice to follow my dreams, make tough decisions that are advantageous for me, have a trusting relationship with GOD, and think positively. When I feel inadequate and unsure of myself, I often remind myself that I am not a victim, perseverance is always with me and that everything that I need is inside of me.

I am Whole

About Marquita Williams

Marquita Williams has served as a healthcare provider over 17 years, published author, and Allied Healthcare professor. She has multiple experiences in leadership, also serving as chair member and subject matter expert for the American Registry for Diagnostic Medical Sonography Organization (or...for a nonprofit organization that administers medical sonography examinations).

A fighter, wife, and mother, with the will to shatter the limitations of all children not having an equal opportunity to succeed. She frequently used her diary to journal and express herself easily and completely, which essentially provided the catharsis needed to navigate through the memories of her erratic childhood and the pain of abandonment, abuse, and rejection. She had endured many hindrances in her life, however success meant resilience, and the desire to pursue her dreams was stronger than the fear of keeping herself hostage to the past.

A career accomplishment she is most proud of, was being asked by successful author Sandra Hagen-Ansert to coauthor the 8th edition of Textbook of Diagnostic Ultrasonography. An ultrasound text book used at radiology sonography programs throughout the United States. She is also most proud of the past 7 years volunteering for the ARDMS organization, where she began working on exam development and now chairs the committee and is a subject matter expert working with a task force with the strategic goal to enhance current assessment programs with cutting edge technology.

Daily prayer, writing in her gratitude journal, and meditation has helped her to step out of the past and begin emitting a strong frequency of vibrating her power into the world. She owes her success to the compassion of her mother and support of her husband.

Early 2017, Marquita founded Lanterns of Hope foundation, a nonprofit devoted to providing mentorship, as well as financial and educational support to low income students, inspiring to become medical sonographers. She is also compassionate about sharing her stories of success and failure with younger generations in her family, as well as challenging and empowering them to find strength in their own adversities and break the glass ceiling of common stereotypes of African-American youth born poor in the projects.

Today she is currently pursuing her master's degree in Management and Leadership at Webster University, has taken the limits off what she thought was impossible, and holds all the abundance that surrounds her life. She is passionate about inspiring other women leaders, as well as taking healthcare to the next level, treating the whole person holistically to promote wellness. She inspires one day to become a world traveler, philanthropist, motivational speaker and renowned best-selling author

CHAPTER 12

7 ESSENTIAL STEPS OF FORGIVENESS

By: Grace L. Holden

Let me share with you my DIRTY life before I became free, as I shared is my first published book DIRTY.

Between the age of 11 – 15 years I was molested repeatedly by my father, for 1 of those years he entered inside of me almost every day or every night; it almost became normal.

Between the age of 11 – 15 years old I was raped by my uncle my dad's brother. He was grimy and drunk and It was disgusting.

Between the age of 15 – 16 years old I was bullied in high school as the ugly duckling.

Between the age of 15-16 years old I was sex-trafficked for almost a year; I ran away and had the age on my ID changed to hide my identity.

At age 17, I became pregnant; and between ages 17 – 18, I was verbally and domestically abused repeatedly by the baby's father. I filed several restraining-orders against him, but I was traumatically stabbed in 4 places, by him. I had very few friends at the time.

Between the age of 19-20, I suffered from posttraumatic stress disorder (PTSD) and was severely depressed, became suicidal right as I was graduating from college. It should have been a triumph success story, but it was an epic failure and disaster.

By the time I turned 21 – I was secretly ashamed no matter what my successes were.

I basically was Dirty, filthy but no one ever knew it. How could I genuinely ever forgive!

I lived a normal life after that, at least it "appeared" normal.

Fast forward, one day when I was 43 years of age, I woke up after a women's retreat event where I had listened to women share, cry and tell their stories (which I never did). I mentored them, prayed with them and even offered counseling services to them. That morning, I said to myself, my dad was controlling me from his grave and I was bound to his decayed corpse in many ways. It began to stink so badly, and his toxins were evidently slowly released into me and I realized I had not ever been free. I was carrying around a weight, dead weight; although often not remembering as much, or even thinking about it daily any more, but I was dragging it around; like a silent victim. The sweet smell of Grace, of my soul begin to fade more and more.

The molestation was just one of the dead weights I was carrying. Dirty stinks. It compromised my senses. It discolored by memory, forgetting the burden I carried. Never to be revealed because I covered in those smelly toxins and dirt much like a pig waddling in a pigpen, content to one's self. Then the mess dried up all over me. Much like many victims I was a slave to the victim mentality. Hidden inside of me was a little girl waiting to have the dirt and scum removed. You see dirt has a very interesting characteristic: when it's all dried up, cleaning it off can work just like an exfoliant. I realized I wasn't supposed to carry failure, discouragement, depression or insecurity.

Ask yourself what are you carrying?

I realized I needed HOPE – I needed strength for my journey or I was going to live the rest of my life full of hidden dirty little secrets and bitterness. I could no longer live with the residue of the trauma and be dead to myself, simply going through the motions of life, pretending like everything was okay.

I had to get beyond Dirty because I desired to live my life without hate or bitterness in my heart. This bitterness and rage would lead to hurting myself more than the people who violated and hurt me. I wanted to spend more time loving on the people who loved me, not less time. I have an older sister who I recently found out was violated by our father also. I didn't know this until I was done writing Dirty and I couldn't speak to her about it because within months of me finding out, she passed away of cancer. I was told that she lived a life that was filled with mood swings and hidden secrets; she shared a space in her life with deep unspeakable pain which often squeezes out the full-time love needed for peace. Also, those around her said it's possible in her subconscious mind she was holding on to the pain of the abuse more than she knew and as she was getting closer to passing, it was clearer as such and revealed through her behavior. No one knows if she forgave him, but what we do know is she did everything to ignore her pain and forget it.

I think back to the times I hid my Dirty little secrets, but no more. The Silence ends, and it ended for me with forgiveness.

Mahatma Gandhi said that, "The weak can never forgive, forgiveness is the attribute of the strong."

I realized how selfish I was being and wanted to share and make a difference to men, women, boys and girls by sharing my story of HOPE. I jumped all in and grew wings as I jumped never to look back. I decided to share my major Dirty little secrets to thousands of people publicly in a 5-video series on Facebook and YouTube; it was an incredible release of fear and liberty. Some people have asked, "How can you still be sane after having faced 5 traumatic life damaging encounters before the age of 20?" One of the core reasons is I forgave.

Nelson Mandela says, "Resentment is like drinking poison and then hoping it will kill your enemies."

Your well-being and good health mentally and physically is necessary for YOU, your family, your community and the nations.

This chapter will focus on the process of Forgiveness: 7 Steps on how to get free, free to be Invincible.

Let me start of by clarifying what forgiveness is NOT:

It's not just for the well-adjusted, happier type of folks

It is not unfathomable, even though is seems like it

It is not weak, foolish, blind, an anomaly or silly submission

It is not automatic

It is not forgetting

Forgiveness is not letting them "off the hook" the saying sticks and stones may break my bones but names will never hurt me; that is NOT true, stick, stones, rocks, violations, breaking of trust, non-protection, molestation, abuse, words, fist and everything I left it DOES hurt.

It is not always easy and it's not always a solo journey

What forgiveness is:

Forgiveness is a learned act

Forgiveness is taking back control

Forgiveness is the essence of strength

Forgiveness deflects negativity

Forgiveness is deliberate release, or it will metastasize like cancer

Forgiveness heals the mind and soothes the heart

Forgiveness is freedom

Forgive them, Forgive You and Win!

Forgiveness is, "me giving up my right to hurt you for hurting me." – unknown

THE PROCESS:

1. **FACE it** - Face the _____(fill in the blank)

What truly happened to you and WHO caused the pain?

For me the blank line was filled with these words; Face the Dirt: Sexual Molestation by my Father, Rape by my Uncle, bullying by mean teenagers, sex-trafficked by scum-bags, verbally and physically abused and stabbed in 4 places – brutal domestic violence, along with a sense of betrayal from loves ones and unprotection by my mother.

How did I do this?

I wrote out a short list just a few words: I hate dad - forgive dad for stealing my innocence and nearly destroying my spirit;

I wrote forgive me (for years I thought I did something to deserve it I asked for it);

I wrote forgive the no name uncle;

I wrote forgive (several girls names – that I won't list here for bullying me);

I wrote and rewrote, erased and barely wrote forgive that man for taking me one day after school and promising to feed me, buy me clothes, do my hair and oh by the way he left out traffic me!

I cried and prayed as I wrote forgive HIM for stabbing me, beating me and tearing be down.

I wrote maybe my mom didn't know better, then I tore up the paper and I found my old journal and I wrote an entire chapter and put it in my book Dirty and I begged God to allow me to forgive her.

I audibly read out each one and was clear on what they did to me and how they made me feel.

What do you need to face?

2. RELEASE it - Release the feelings of what you listed in step 1.

For me I had to release the DIRT. The violence, anger, humiliation and rage associated with it. It was a process for me to dismiss it. Saying the words, even writing the words was much easier than releasing the weight, bitter, pain, and rage I often felt that was beyond words. This included releasing the passive attitude I sometimes had and releasing the forgetfulness I sometimes carried. When you release it with your words, your heart and your core inner place, you can begin to release the toxins that cause the extreme emotions of brokenness, fury or depression. Although, as humans these may be normal at a reasonable level until they become dangerous to your life and health and fuel your wellbeing. When the stress of your emotions compromises your health (physical and mental) it can turn into a stress disorder and long-term effects could take place. To avoid or minimize this altogether- RELEASE it. Don't carry it around.

3. CONFRONT it – This may be one of the hardest part of the process.

This step requires some courage dealing with the people responsible or those who were irresponsible for what has happened to you.

Use caution and wisdom during this stage. Addressing the accused, the victimizers, people who devalued you in a manner that is responsible sometimes is hard to imagine. Ever seen a case where the family member of a victim who may not be able to speak for themselves and the judge says this is your opportunity to make a statement to the accused; often the room has to prepare for not only the verbal retaliation and rage that may present itself, but the physical act of an attack or violent response towards the person being accused. With so many emotions happening anything is liable to pop off or go down in the court room. Sometimes resulting in the arrest of the angered victim's family member.

This is another time in the process where you will need to use your words and writing them for clarity will be important. In addition, seeking guidance on how to do this step from your loved ones you trust, a support system or support group, a trusted friend, from professionals who are trained to help you will make this step more navigable. I remember when I reached this step, I was grateful I didn't have to face my father because he had died almost 20 years prior. I was also upset because he wasn't around to own what he did to me and hear my pain, make amends. However, for some of the people who hurt me, it would never be an option for me to confront them. Although they are alive for me to, it was not safe nor was it feasible. Take a moment to write down who you want to confront even if you are unable to for whatever reason, write their name on paper, fold it and destroy it in a manner you feel comfortable. Do not plan to keep it or carry it around.

Forgiveness is an act of the will, and the will can function regardless of the temperature of your heart – Corneten Boom

4. **FORGIVE Yourself** – It's important to not cast blame on yourself, beat you up and internalize guilt or shame associated with the pain or harm done to you.

Unpleasant memories often require coping strategies beyond the scope of one able to just do it automatically on your own. It's okay to seek help to process, get rid of any guilt or shame of an unpleasant memory. Sometimes FEAR is so real it is disabling. Remember you are NOT the one who did the victimizing. Sometimes triggers remind you of the event. For example, in my case a sound, a smell or for some just a thought or another painful traumatic moment. Forgiving yourself for varying reasons may be necessary. If you do not need this step that is excellent, you can concentrate more on the next step.

5. **RECOGNIZE the fallout** – in the 5th step you will look at what happened as a result of ignoring the pain, not releasing the pain, nor confronting it, or even blaming yourself.

Often the real question in this step is to ask yourself, "What did you turn to? With your attitude, actions or behavior. For some of us we turned to depression, others loneliness, many to stress, often comprising who you really are, in some cases, alcoholism, drugs or excessive habits; extreme sadness or work alcoholic (the last one was me). This is a good place to resolve bad relationships that resulted from recognizing what you may have propelled yourself toward. Identify cycles of repeated behavior. Ever said to yourself why does it seem like you are a magnet to bad karma or energy? This step is the realization of that vicious cycle. This is not always easy and often almost impossible to truly recognize. Don't give up on this step. You will have a real moment with you in this step. Don't beat yourself up, be honest and genuine with yourself.

6. **FORGIVE the Accused** – It was quoted through Oprah who heard someone say that forgiveness is giving up the hope that the past could have been any different.

In this step you digest, not ingest the past, move forward, rediscover your true you.

Fall in Love with You (F.L.Y) and get You back!!

To forgive is to see a prisoner free and discover that the answer was you!!

~Louis B. Smedes.

You take control here. The name (s) you wrote down and folded it; don't simply put it in the trash - destroy it, burn it and bury it!! Physically go outside, dig a hole and bury the ashes. I had the opportunity last year to go through a Forgiveness Ceremony with an awesome God sent woman named Alva Tate. The most important thing I retained from the awesome experience is you can't dig back up what you release, destroy and bury.

7. **CELEBRATE you and** heal – The 7th step is not to be skipped or circumvented.

How do you celebrate you?

You can celebrate you alone or with friends and loved ones but most importantly make it a big deal and celebrate. I went on a mini-trip after going through the process and I also recognized I needed to do the steps a few times, repeat – wash – rinse and SMILE. I was thankful for the victory and celebrating it improved my self-esteem, my outlook on what was ahead of me and reminded me why I could never go back to the unforgiving state I was previously in.

In conclusion, I wish for no one to get destination disease. Forgiveness isn't just a destination, it's a journey – a way of life. I haven't fully arrived yet; however, I am well on the journey and it's a journey I do not want to travel alone.

Will you join me?

Do you have secrets you need to share?

Are you ready to begin the process to forgive?

If so, I am here for you, reach out to be on my Grace L Holden site and let's forgive together.

To NOT forgive is abusing the abused ~ Coreena Brown

With Love, Grace

About Grace Holden

Author Grace L. Holden is a mother of 5, a lover of people. She was the Victim of multiple traumas before the age of 20! She is a Voice of HOPE sharing her incredible story delivered in the most unique, brilliant and transparent way.

Grace is a multi-passionate Keynote Motivational Speaker, Leadership Expert, and Personal & Executive Coach whose unwavering sense of dedication and no-nonsense approach have earned her the reputation as a down-to- earth strategist in the business space. Throughout the span of over two decades, she has garnered extensive expertise helping people thrive both professionally and personally.

Grace is an unstoppable visionary and a positive force. During her undergraduate years at Seattle Pacific University, Grace was severely abused, stabbed and oppressed...and those weren't even her worst traumas. Through all the seemingly life ending repeated devastations, Grace refused to quit and somehow managed to complete her undergraduate degree in Communications while being a single mother.

Currently, Grace proudly serves as the Founder and CEO of a personal and professional growth and development company called Real Champions League, LLC. She is known intimately for her mastery of Inspirational Storytelling. For the last decade, Grace was the Host of a prominent annual Women's Unity Conference in Las Vegas helping to free the lives of thousands.

Watch for her next yarn weaver "Dark" the journey to Dirty. She is also writing other inspirational books entitled "Extraordinaire You" and "F.L.Y" First Love Yourself where she spills the tea on Depression that most people ignore.

Prior to her present ventures, Grace owned a successful professional counseling business for many years and worked as an Executive of Training and Development for a major corporation. In addition to a Master's Degree in Human Services, she holds a Certified John Maxwell Coach, Trainer, Speaker, and Leader designation. Ultimately, Grace is on a lifelong mission to empower people to find their unique voice, discover their passion, and unlock their hidden potential.

Grace has a heart big enough to fit the world in it and she has the tenacity to be the Catalyst of a Nationwide Movement – Dads Against Dirty (DADS).

Grace is destined to unify men and women, boys and girls, survivors, concerned organizations and other authors to help bring awareness to the trauma many hide. Join Grace in her dedication and commit to the cause.

CHAPTER 13

RISE FROM THE ASHES

By: Jackie Morey

"And endurance develops strength of character, and character strengthens our confident hope of salvation. And this hope will not lead to disappointment. For we know how dearly God loves us, because he has given us the Holy Spirit to fill our hearts with his love." Romans 5:4~5 NLT

Ground Zero

In December 2014, the church community that my family belonged to, experienced something excruciating.

The Senior Pastor and his wife were asked to resign because of things we had no idea that they had done and words they had spoken over the course of 15 years.

Their actions and words had deeply hurt scores of families – from Parents, and even their children, who had been attending the K-12 school that the Church community had established. These children had grown up in this loving and close-knit community since birth, and now they were in their teens or 20s.

Unfortunately, the leadership, namely the Senior Pastor and his wife had created a culture of religious legalism, without the "amazing grace" that they preached. After the Senior Pastor resigned, families left the church community in droves. Hundreds felt emotionally abused, manipulated and disgusted with anything that had to do with "church."

My Husband and I were in deep shock and couldn't believe that the entire thing unraveled so quickly, right before our eyes.

The remaining Pastors and Elders did their best to stop the hemorrhaging. If I were to use a word picture, it would be like trying to stop the bleeding from a person who had been violently stabbed in the heart.

After the Pastors and Elders met with as many families as possible who wanted to ask questions, vent, and give them feedback – the good, the bad, and the ugly, the Pastoral leadership decided not to fold the church as an organization, and instead, continue under the same name, and serve whoever decided to stay.

As part of the solution to get some relief from the grief and the pain, the Eldership wisely held three back-to-back evening worship services led by well-known Worship Leader Jason Upton.

Indeed, many people we hadn't seen in months showed up during those three nights. But it was nowhere near the size of the original congregation.

Each night Jason Upton did a phenomenal job of leading everyone into worship and the presence of God, a place that we hadn't experienced before. It was different. It was fresh. There was no familiarity – the negative kind.

I'm talking about the negative kind of familiarity wherein the Lord Jesus Himself could do no miracles because of the town's unbelief.

Why were they in unbelief? Because they knew Him when He was still little. They knew Him as the carpenter, Joseph's son. They knew His mother, and brothers and sisters. That's the kind of familiarity I'm talking about. The negative kind.

So, during those three precious nights of worship – where the negative type of familiarity wasn't welcome, I believe many people were profoundly touched by God's Spirit – and some emotional healing took place.

And yet the damage was so deep and so wide that this wasn't enough.

A few months went by.

Then in June 2015, the Pastoral leadership decided that a name change and a fresh look, i.e. a remodeling of the Altar area would help our community.

Most of us remained hopeful that this decision would draw more of our former church community back, and perhaps even draw in new people.

We were excited to see what would happen.

Well, we went through the name change, which was actually a very beautiful and hope-filled name. And we went through the remodel.

We waited several more months to see if our community would grow.

But week after week, the atmosphere in the community didn't change much. It certainly wasn't the same as it had been before December 2014. In fact, it was never the same again.

My Husband and I felt the heaviness, the grief, the apathy, and the complacency of our community – those of us who remained.

Another "bombshell" occurred when in early December 2015, our Pastoral leadership announced that December 24, 2015 – Christmas Eve service – would be the final service of our church community – the sparse hundred or so who remained.

They also conveyed that on December 31, 2015, the church entity would cease to exist.

That was the final blow.

Our small community was devastated. We had held on to hope for a year, hope that we would recover. Hope that the families who had been hurt by the former Senior Pastor and his wife, would return, now that they were gone.

This never happened.

Who knows why?

Perhaps because the foundation had been irreparably damaged, and the Lord wanted to "burn it to the ground," so to speak.

And this way, we could all start fresh – elsewhere.

The Fallout

In the months that followed, we learned first-hand, as well as heard some jaw-dropping, shocking and heart-wrenching stories about what the Senior Pastor and his wife did and said to people, or talked to others about these people.

Most of it was manipulative, mentally abusive and emotionally abusive. And all of it was soul-crushing, demoralizing, and quite disturbing.

It was so abominable, loathsome and detestable that it caused family rifts.

For example, young adult children who had graduated from the K-12 Academy refused to be involved in any church community, especially whichever community their parents chose to belong to after the church blew out.

Others young adults completely gave up on any relationship with God.

Some Husband-Wife relationships became incredibly strained.

Why?

Because of what had been done to them personally by the Senior Pastor and his wife and also because their children had turned away from the Lord.

We Drank the Kool-Aid

According to Wikipedia, "**Drinking the Kool-Aid** is an idiom commonly used in the United States that refers to any person or group who goes along with a doomed or dangerous idea because of peer pressure."

Well, I drank the Kool-Aid. And my Husband drank it, too.

As we both looked back over the many years we had been part of the now-defunct church community, we had many A-HA moments as it dawned on us some red flags that were there along the way.

For example, we incredulously decided that the annual 5-Day long Family Camp – which the entire church community planned for many months in advance to participate in, and everyone took vacation days for – was more important than attending the wedding of my Husband's niece in Canada!

It wasn't even a question in our minds that we had to be at Family Camp. We were going to be at Family Camp. Period. Nothing would deter us from this. Not even our niece's wedding.

Oh my. How could we have been so blind?!

Simple. It's because we had drunk the Kool-Aid!

Here's another red flag.

How about the fact that we didn't have much time to make friends with those outside the church community because we were so heavily involved in the many, many church community activities and events.

For example, there weren't just the Sunday services. There were Thursday night Home Groups, which were required for every family who had children in the K-12 Academy, monthly

Women's meetings, Quarterly Conferences, Leadership meetings, Prayer meetings, the list goes on and on!

Now let me be clear. Our church community was made up of the most caring, hospitable, committed and Christ-centered people we had ever met. Our friendships were strong, deep and healthy.

And yet we had all – yes, they and we – had all drunk the Kool-Aid. We rarely questioned the Senior Pastor or his wife because then we'd be labeled as, "rebellious."

See how that worked?

We failed to see clearly.

We failed to stop and discern. We failed to listen to those outside our community. We failed each other. We failed our families. We failed our friends.

Rise from the Ashes

When our Official church community entity ceased to exist effective December 31, 2015, my Husband and I were crushed.

We were emotionally worn out, we were devastated, we felt waves of grief and loss crash over us, and I personally went into 2016 going through the ups and downs of the grieving process.

Well, we decided that we didn't want to stay in this place, to stay stuck, or to hardly make much forward progress.

We decided that part of our healing process was to purposefully find a Sozo minister in our area.

Sozo is a ministry that originated from Bethel Church in Redding, California.

[Note: Bethel Church has trained and mentored Sozo Teams from all over the world.]

Sozo is the Greek word which means "salvation."

And this doesn't only include the salvation of one's spirit; it also includes the salvation of one's soul – one's mind, one's will and one's emotions from excruciating wounds to one's mind, will and emotions.

In other words, Sozo means "to be made whole." To be made whole after one experiences deep pain, huge loss, emotional trauma, physical trauma, and mental trauma.

After we found a Sozo Team – who happened to be at a church community over 3 hours away, my Husband and I hired a nanny for that appointed day, we took her and our kids with us, and we made the trek to the Sozo teams in Port Angeles, Washington.

We had no idea what would happen, since it was our very first Sozo session.

My Husband Jim had his session with two Sozo team members in one room, and I had my own Sozo session with two other team members in another room.

Oh, my goodness!! What we each experienced during our individual two-hour Sozo sessions was extraordinary, glorious and astonishing!

The session also included actively and out-loud forgiving the Senior Pastor and his wife. It involved hearing what God was saying to us, it also involved being immersed in GOD's presence the entire time!

Amazingly, I felt the weight of the grief and the low-grade pain of all the losses – all lift off from me. There's no question in my mind, that this was a supernatural experience, and I was free!

My Husband and I were both free – free from grief, free from the pain of deep, deep loss, and free to face the future with a renewed sense of hope and freedom.

Oh, Freedom.

What a remarkable gift from the Lord!!

And yet this was only the beginning!

On January 1, 2017, as we were driving back to Seattle suburbia from a family reunion in Santa Cruz, California – the Lord gave my Husband an impression.

I'll paraphrase the impression he received from the Lord, which he later shared with me.

"This year, I want you and Jackie to become new wineskins because I am going to pour new wine into you both."

Before I move on, do you know why new wine shouldn't be poured into old wineskins back when they still used animal skins for wine?

Well, it's because <u>new wine</u> ferments. And if a person poured new wine into an <u>old wineskin,</u> because old wineskins are brittle – the fermentation process would cause the old wineskin to burst. And the person would lose both the wineskin and the wine.

And this is why new wine must only be poured into new wineskins.

Well, on July 9, 2017, I experienced the beginning of an exceptionally remarkable transformation.

I had signed up for a 7-Day Life On Fire Challenge which helped me get clear on my 6-month Vision, and set me up to clarify my top 3 Personal and top 3 Professional goals.

Two weeks later, after I had successfully completed the 7-Day Challenge, I enrolled in the Life On Fire Coaching Academy to become a Transformational, Breakthrough and Performance Coach!!

Then at the beginning of August 2017, I attended a 4-day event called "Abundance" which was also where my entire way of being so decidedly and radically shifted.

Talk about becoming a <u>new wineskin</u> – I most certainly became one.

When I got home from the Abundance event, my Husband noticed such a tremendous difference in me, that he signed himself up for the next 7-Day Life On Fire Challenge, which was at the end of August!

Great News: He experienced an amazingly far-reaching transformation that he signed up for Life On Fire Momentum Coaching – which is an Accountability coaching program.

With Momentum Coaching, my Husband has also shifted his way of being.

And I can now say that the Lord orchestrated all of this, and that we have both been wonderfully and marvelously transformed.

Indeed, **he became a new wineskin**, and **I became a new wineskin**.

At present, I'm well on my way to becoming a successful Transformational, Breakthrough and Performance Coach.

Would you like to know what distinguishes me from tens of thousands of Coaches out there?

Well, what makes me unique is that I believe in the prophetic, I believe in the supernatural. And that the source of the prophetic is the Lord Jesus Christ Himself.

And because I pray for all my Clients, I believe that whenever HE chooses to, I can hear God share His thoughts and "secrets" about them, with me. And I plan on not simply coaching them at a level that tens of thousands of other coaches could serve them at.

As I pray for all my Clients fervently and seek the heart and the mind of God about them, I am in a position to receive words of knowledge, words of wisdom and the prophetic flow for them specifically. Words that could completely change their lives!

Now isn't that game-changing?

Final Thoughts

So, you see, from the depths of grief and loss, from the gripping pain of failure, from the awful decision to "Drink the Kool-Aid" year after year – I have risen from the ashes and have become an extraordinarily transformed woman.

I'm a new wineskin, not an old one.

What about you?

Have you experienced unbelievable failure?

Have you gone through excruciating pain, trauma, breakdowns?

Well, dear one – you can move the needle forward from failure, pain, grief, trauma, sorrow, and loss...to healing, deliverance, freedom and transformational success.

Whatever life throws your way, you can decide and commit to move from fear to freedom, from loss to supernatural gain, from trauma to transformational success.

Indeed – YOU can become INVINCIBLE.

Here's my parting thought for you: "Live a life of significance and leave your legendary legacy." ~Jackie Morey

About Jackie Morey

Jackie Morey is a premier entrepreneur, multiple #1 International Bestselling Author, and Business and Transformational Coach extraordinaire. She's also a Book Publisher, and the Founder and CEO of Customer Strategy Academy.

Her passion is to help authors, coaches, business professionals, and entrepreneurs, grow their business & live their life purposefully to succeed thrive, and flourish through her Coaching, Book Publishing, and Online Marketing businesses.

As a degreed Engineer, she brings her unique logical expertise to simplify the nuts and bolts of self-publishing her mission is to help you grow your business & live your life on purpose.

She's happily married and lives in a beautiful Pacific Northwest suburb of Seattle with her husband Jim. They have a son and a daughter who "make them proud" every day.

Jackie Morey can be contacted at:

www.JackieMorey.com

www.facebook.com/JackieMorey777

www.LinkedIn.com/in/JackieMorey1

www.Twitter.com/JackieMorey1

CHAPTER 14

BECOMING AN INVINCIBLE WARRIOR

By: Dr. Cornelia Wenze

The main purpose of writing this story is to share my experience of exposure to challenging situations that were the catalysts to becoming an invincible warrior. I experienced domestic violence in the home as a child, the death of a parent as a young adult, financial setbacks, and educational hurdles. I also had the privilege of watching my mother transition from a full-time homemaker to the role of a single mother after the untimely death of my father.

All of us have had life experiences that were both good and bad. Yet, in spite of my challenges I have not only excelled but prevailed. My life began in Fitzgerald, Georgia on September 9, 1964. I was the second child born to Alberta and Ira Wenze. My parent's first daughter passed away before I was born. After my birth, my parents had four other children, which included three boys and another girl. My younger sister was the product of a stillborn birth. I became my parents' only surviving daughter.

My three brothers and I grew up in a middle-class home environment. My father was a medical doctor and my mother a housewife, who later became a teacher. I was fortunate to grow up in a two-parent household. We lived in a nice neighborhood, went to great schools, experienced family vacations, and were exposed to great comforts, as children.

Some might have concluded that my family and I lived a privileged lifestyle free of challenges. After all, we lived in a nice neighborhood and our home was adequately furnished. Both of my parents had nice automobiles which included a sports car and a recreational vehicle. My family had a housekeeper who cleaned the home, babysat, and prepared meals.

My family was just like all typical upper middle-class family, at the time. From outward appearance, everyone likely presumed that my home life was fantastic. My brothers and I attended school daily. We were always clean and dressed in the best clothes. We had enough school supplies. We could eat anything we wanted. When we asked for money it was given to us. It all sounds too good to be true, right? Well the fairytale, as I've shared ends now.

You should know that my father was not much of a communicator and spent countless hours in his bedroom with the television on when he was not working. I suppose it is safe to say that my father was isolative and preferred to be alone when he was present in the home.

My mother was the glue that kept the family together. She did everything for the well-being of her children. However, at times my father took the role my mother played in the home for granted. Let me add that he was often condescending and combative towards my mother.

I remember being a young child and witnessing my father display physical aggression towards my mother. Yes, I know this is shocking to phantom that a doctor, father, husband, and pillar of the community was abusive. I was initially shocked and thought this was a one-time incident. Yet, it was not, and the domestic violence continued for years throughout their marriage.

When I took up for my mother, I became a victim of my father's abuse. He never hit me, but I experienced verbal abuse. I recall being told I was "stupid" and would never amount to anything in life. Besides the endless support of my mother, as well as my desire to get my doctorate, being told I was stupid was engrained in my mind at times during the pursuit of my education. I suppose it is safe to say that the little girl in me, who grew up being called stupid had this blazing desire to prove her father wrong. I had to become someone and the Warrior in me became Dr. Cornelia

Wenze. Imagine, if I let this traumatic experience of being exposed to domestic violence impede my willingness to press forward and overcome this hurdle.

My father passed away unexpectedly when I was a junior in college. At that time, I was in college and had more of a party minded mindset instead of being education focused. Now the warrior in me had to make some decisions. I considered my mother who had three teenage children and had just become a widow. It would not be fair to her or my siblings, if I continued to party in college and not focus on my educational goals.

A shift took place and the Warrior within me became education focused. I realized that I no longer had the financial support from my father. My new reality did not include my father as the primary breadwinner any longer. My father was deceased, and this impacted my family in a huge manner.

However, not succeeding was never an option for me. I remember after my father's burial my mother told me to return to college and get it done. She assured me that she and my brothers would be just fine. I did as she instructed me to, although I had some mixed emotions.

Throughout my college years I did incur some challenges that could have produced a negative outcome if I had not been resilient. In graduate school I had a committee member who would not sign off on my internship without a letter of completion from the supervisor. Well the supervisor of my internship took a year to write me a letter of completion. Needless to say I met my graduate requirements and graduated with my masters. The invincible Warrior in me refused to quit or give up in spite of the setback.

At the time of his death, my father was a practicing physician. My mother became a widow in her forties. Life changed for her in an instant. Sadly, my father did not have his finances in order prior to his death and left my mother in a financial quandary.

My mother discovered after my father passed away that he had cancelled all his insurance policies. He also had some unresolved financial issues at that time. My mother was more of a housewife at the time and had not worked professionally for several years. She assisted with some office duties in my dad's practice when he was alive but hadn't worked competitively.

My mother not only became a widow but the single parent of three teenage boys. How does a person transition from a wife and mother to a dual role of mother and dad? I know it was not easy for her. At the time of my dad's death my mother resided in Georgia and had no support system. She decided to re-locate to her home town of Miami, Florida where she had a support system in place.

My mother had to make some quick decisions in order to provide for her family. Now remember my dad did not leave her in a great financial position. Therefore, she sold my dad's private practice. Initially, when my mother returned to Miami she resided with her parent's and my two younger brothers lived with me in Tallahassee where I was a college student. My other brother entered the military after his high school graduation. In addition, he discovered that he would become a teenage parent.

I can only imagine what emotions my mother may have been experiencing during this period in her life. I am sure she was sad due to my father's untimely death. She probably was embarrassed at the position my father left her in. My mother may have been angry at my father as well. I am sure she might have been afraid because she is now a widow who is responsible for raising teenage boys alone.

Well my mother became an invincible Warrior and her survival skills kicked in and she returned to the work force. My mother had an associate's degree and decided to enter the education field and became employed as a substitute teacher. She personified strength for my two teenage brothers who were in the home with her. My brothers witnessed my mother embrace her challenges and transform from a homemaker to the primary breadwinner of her household. My mother is my hero and I followed her example to raise a young man as a single parent.

In 1996, I discovered that I was pregnant with my son. Now, let's discuss my pregnancy a little. At the time I conceived my son, I was not married. Oh yes, the taboo of being pregnant and not married. I was 32 years old with a career when I got pregnant. I could not fathom why it was such a big deal that I was pregnant out of wedlock. It was an exciting moment in my life when I became the proud parent of my one and only favorite son, Khadeem Wilson, in 1997. He has brought so much delight to my life and made parenting a wonderful experience.

My mother set the standard for me on how to raise an honorable young man. I witnessed her at a distance raise my brothers who became exemplary men. In addition, my mother retired when my son was a baby to assist me with his upbringing as a single mother. In essence she stepped out of her single parent role into that of a caretaker of my young son.

The torch was passed from my mother to me and the stage was set for me to embrace my transition into the world of being a single parent to a male child. The invincible Warrior inside me became unleashed. In becoming an invincible Warrior self-discovery had to take place. It was important that I knew who I was. I had to ask myself who am I? The real me had to be awaken.

We as women are sometimes told that we cannot raise a boy to be a man. Yet, some of us are thrust into this dual role of being a mother and a father. I think for me the father role outweighed the mother role on many occasions. In my case I nurtured my son as mothers do but I also was authoritative as fathers do.

Let's just say my son got the best of both worlds from the perspective of a mother. Naysayers please be quiet. I know some of you are already voicing opinions without letting me finish my story. Yes, it is my story from my perspective.

I will admit as a single mother I questioned if I adequately met the needs of my son at times. I worked non-stop because I was the primary breadwinner. Yet, I made sure my son's basic needs were met. In addition, I made sure I was involved in his life in spite of any mayhem that occurred in my life.

I never let challenges I experienced in my life impact my son's life. Was this an easy task? N, it was not. How can one not let their complications spill over into their role as a parent? For me it was important to ensure that my son remained emotionally healthy. That meant my drama was not his drama. Parents keep your child out of your adult business.

On becoming an invincible warrior please do not try to give the appearance of a perfect person, who is not broken or has inadequacies. You know that person who says, "I am happy, secure, and my life is perfect." This person looks good externally and would make some envious of their perfect life.

Look in the mirror and awaken to the real you. The real you have blemishes, imperfections, wounds, scars, shortcomings, pain, fears, and disappointments and this is okay. The problem is that some individuals prefer not to accept their true selves and give an illusion of who they really are. Why is this a fact?

Well, it could be that an individual has no idea of who they are and accepts others' interpretations. The goal is to accept your total self. The process of becoming an invincible Warrior can only take place after one accepts who they really are internally and externally. Begin to change your way of thinking and start to embrace all of you.

After you discover who you are develop a winner mindset on the path to becoming an invincible Warrior. Maintaining the proper mindset is vital. It is important to understand that we dictate who we are. Your thoughts become words and your words become actions.

Learn to control your mind. Tell your mind what it needs to do instead of letting it control you. Remember you are who you think you are. You are a winner, or you are a failure. The choice is yours. When you struggle with a situation, you can accept your mental state surrounding it or control your thoughts. Begin to train your mind to think of optimistic affirmations. State out boldly, "I am worthy of better days. I am valuable. I am prosperous."

I have encountered situations in life that were consuming and mind-boggling. During these challenging periods, I felt as if I was coming apart at the seams. My inner being was consumed. The difficulties I encountered were suffocating, and I felt that no end was near.

The mind is one of the biggest minefields in life. We are constantly at war with what goes on inside of our headspace. It can be anger, sadness, fear, anxiety, regret, etc. The victory or the loss, as well as success and failure, are all determined in the mind. If an individual can conquer their mental thoughts, they can become an invincible Warrior.

It is important for an invincible Warrior to have a diligent prayer life. It is the belief of many people that there is power in prayer. Prayer expands faith and leaves us with expectancy in our souls. I expect positive changes to occur in my life and I refuse to give up.

God wants the believer to be dependent on Him for needs that can only be met by Him. On countless occasions, I had to pray and maintain faith in what I knew only God could do. I have noticed that my mental battles diminish due to the strength and consistency of my prayer life.

Learn to embrace who you are. Remember, the real you, has some scars, bruises, pain, disappointments, and blemishes. When you become authentic, you accept all of who you really are. Change your mindset to that of positivity. You are the master of you.

We all have within us the capacity to overcome and not accept defeat. We can evolve beyond our difficulties. Obstacles are inevitable and will arise. An invincible Warrior overcomes mayhem, challenges, chaos, and setbacks. I overcame witnessing domestic violence as a child. I overcame the death of my father as a young adult. I overcame financial setbacks and educational hurdles. I overcame the challenges of single parenting a male child. The time is now to ignite the Warrior on the inside of us. Be open to becoming an invincible Warrior.

About Dr. Cornelia Wenze

Dr. Cornelia Wenze purpose and passion is to connect people to a process that embraces the now what moment during chaotic times. She grew up in a middle-class home environment and was raised by both parents. Dr. Wenze is the eldest and only girl of four siblings. She was always a dreamer as a child and aspired to become a doctor. Dr. Wenze received a doctorate in counseling psychology in 2003 and has over 27 years' experience as a mental health professional. The proudest moment of her life was the birth of her one and only favorite son, Khadeem Wilson.

Dr. Wenze is a non-judgmental mental health practitioner with an eclectic style. Her continued goal is to provide services in her community that is as healthy for her as it is for clients she serves. Dr. Wenze's desire is to enable individuals she serves to transform and have an optimum life. All her previous work in the mental health field provided the foundation for a new role as an author and motivational speaker. Her current literary work is Transformation Through Chaos Making a Setback a Comeback. Her next literary project is Invincible How to Embrace Failure and Achieve Transformational Success.

Dr. Wenze has established platforms through networking and speaking to inspire and motivate others. She has connected with several churches, community agencies, as well as professional organizations. Dr. Wenze is a resourceful, divine, and devoted promoter who proactively markets her services and advocates for those seeking to be inspired. She speaks nationally at churches, schools, businesses, and conferences. Connect with her at Transformationthroughchaos.com.

CHAPTER 15

AWAKENING

By: Dr. Jessica Vera

Have you ever wondered, "Am I fully awake...?" This question might seem odd, but if you have never had the opportunity to speak with an individual, who had a near-death experience, then you might be surprised by what you discovered from their process, about yourself. A near-death experience, what is that? Some say, death is defined by a lack of brain activity. Yet, others, more philosophical might say, it's when life ceases to have meaning. For me, throughout my life, I've had moments that seemed to me, as near-death experiences. The definition that I arrived at for these types of experiences may not be collectively understood. But here it is, being near-death has meant being fully aware in the moment that everything that I treasured on this earth, could in an instant vanish, be taken away. Your body gasping for oxygen, realizing that you don't have control over it and even your thoughts are no longer your own. A very unpleasant and unsettling experience really. Who would want to experience that right? In January of 2017, after a great deal of introspective reflection and evaluation, I made the conscious decision to seek a near-death experience with purpose.

I was born in Lima, Peru, but was not raised in my country of origin. Rather I was an import to North America, Canada. I lived my youth in Canada. Fell in love in Canada. Gave birth to several successful businesses in Canada. Found my true love and gave birth to my first child in Canada. Yet, I never really felt connected to the culture in Canada. As God would have it, I've since lived the last 20 years, in Florida. A far cry from the culture in Canada, but somewhat more like what it might have been like to grow-up in Peru. Florida is where I gave birth to my second child and found my calling.

People live their entire lives roaming the earth, interacting with others, accumulating and achieving things in life, but never really living. I've always asked myself, "Why would anyone want to exist in this way." That is until the fall of 2015, when my existence, as I had known it up until that point in my life, came to a screeching halt. My past caught up with my present and began to threaten my future. It was time to face demons I had tried to outrun. It's funny, you don't realize how much of a guise you created for yourself, until you are confronted with undeniable truth. Existence no longer is sufficient, because you are changing, maturing, evolving into what God had created and intended for you all along, but you were just too resistant to accept because it looked nothing like what you would have chosen for yourself. So, the awakening begins.

The plane landed in Lima, Peru. I had been advised on how to take care of myself in this foreign land, because tourists unfortunately are prime targets for the impoverished and criminals. Walking among my country men and women felt weird, unfamiliar, yet somehow more connected than I had felt in years, at home. Then after a few hours, we were back on a plane headed for the interior of the country, The Amazon. Picture this a five-foot-two-inch petite woman, lugging two full size suitcases, filled with all the comforts of home, but that would prove totally useless in the environment I would shortly find myself. Onlookers snickering in amusement at the "Gringa," whose appearance was more like their own, than that of a white foreigner, but whose behavior was like something out of a comedy. Finally, we arrive...

How do you know that you are fully alive? Is it a feeling? Is it based upon what others perceive of you? Or simply that there is oxygenated blood flowing through your veins. I've worked with people my entire professional career, helping them feel alive, transforming the seemingly dead, into vibrant beings. And it has been my experience that the distinction between a thriving living soul, and a shell, starts with acceptance of Grace and Love. Like every living being on this planet, I've experienced my share of Pain, at the hands of those who should have protected me or at least respected me. These types of painful experiences leave deep scars.

Scars that are not easily erased, but that influence one's very essence in an insidious and sometimes not very subtle way. We do all that we know to eradicate it's influence over us, but the demons are powerful beyond belief.

How do you know that you are fully alive? Simple because you are not dead yet.

Here I was in a wooden box, much like what a coffin might appear like from the inside, only I had a little more comfort. A bed made of planks and a very thin, what I suspect was supposed to be a mattress and a wooden chair and table. No protection from the elements or the wildlife. Just air breezing through the open rafters. Nightfall arrived before expected, and then it was time. I would embark upon a near-death journey of my choosing. Why? Because throughout my life there were a few gifted skills I had mastered and one of them was mind-control. This might sound peculiar, but one of the gifts of surviving sexual abuse, is the ability to compartmentalize. I can choose what I will allow into my conscious mind and control it and my associated feelings, while repressing the rest. Consequently, hypnosis and traditional regressive work had never been effective options for me.

I was provided a substance to drink, it was gulped, because it was disgusting in taste. Later I would find out that the amount I was given was far too much for my frame and constitution. A human scientist by inquisitiveness I had studied all modern thought about the human psyche and its outward impact on behavior, but now I felt ready to explore ancient practices, and I chose the practices of the Shipibo people. This ancient tribal tradition partaking in ceremonial plant medicine was part of my extended heritage and having researched it extensively, at least to the extent permitted by the remaining 20,000 tribal members, it provided a means to unlock repressed memories buried many years ago.

Do you recall a movie and subsequent television series called the, "Twilight Zone?" If you don't it was [I believe it still continues to be on air], a visual representation of altered realities experienced through the eyes of simple humans. Everything that I had read about Ayahuasca had been clear as mud, that's a pun, because when prepared authentically, that is what the brew looks like, mud. Now there is something that I must make very clear, I had never taken any type of drug that was mood or consciousness altering in my life. In fact, taking medication in general had never been a proponent of my philosophy for treatment. However, this ancient practice intrigued me, due to the season of my life. It was time to face my demons head on.

The main ingredient of this brew is a vine, Banisteriopsis caapi, which like the tea itself is also called ayahuasca (which means 'vine of the soul' or 'vine with a soul'). The secondary ingredient is either chacruna (Psychotria viridis) or chagropanga (Diplopterys cabrerana), plants that contain a relatively high amount of the psychedelic substance DMT.

Here is what is written about its origin, "First recorded Western contact with ayahuasca was made in 1851 by Richard Spruce, the famous ethnobotanist from England. When considering archeological evidence of comparable native plant use, it seems likely that its use dates back to at least two millennia ago." Ayahuasca can induce a psychedelic, visionary state of mind. Shamans or 'medicine men' take ayahuasca to communicate with nature or to see what is causing a patient's illness on a spiritual level. Drinking ayahuasca and singing together takes them into a healing and inspiring kind of trance.

Ayahuasca has slowly been gaining interest from Western society not only by academic researchers in the field of psychotherapy but also by 'Psychonauts', "People who practice responsible and conscious use of mind-altering substances, use ayahuasca to confront themselves with the richness of the mind, the infinity of the universe, and their deepest fears, so as to experience ecstasy resulting from facing and overcoming these fears."

I lay still, on a thin yoga mat, in surroundings that were partitioned by a beautiful Palapa hut. To my left a young girl, who was obviously struggling with some serious demons. I thought to myself, "Does she really know what she is getting herself into, or is this just another trip for her, not unlike the thousands she had taken in the past, to escape, escape what she would later share was repeated abuse and exploitation and self-deprecation." To my right, an open passage way to the outside. I thought to myself, "Perfect if this was a mistake then I can simply get up and walk out."

I felt nothing, saw nothing, started to get frustrated that all the anticipation of what would be revealed, unmasked and recovered was nothing more than an unfulfilled deserve. Time seemed to stand still, I could hear my heart beating, the sounds of others around me moaning and talking, chanting and singing. There was an aroma of flowers that surrounding me, but also the sting of purging and cleansing. This was becoming another unproductive experience of gaining further insight to battle my demons.

Awakening is time-released. It does not impose itself, but rather is polite and waits for an invitation. There are times when we think we want the answers to questions that have plagued our life and likely stifled out potential, but until we are truly ready to accept responsibility for our choices, awakening sits patiently in the alcoves of our mind. Fear tends to be the principle obstacle between knowing and continuing to allow life to live us, rather than living life as we were ordained is the preference of most humans on this planet.

Initially everything was black and white, lots of geometric shapes, but no color. Then as if, someone turned on the switch to illumination, I began to see in my mind's eye all that had been hidden deep beneath the surface. Memories that were repressed for good reason. I watched in horror, while my body involuntarily began to protect itself. I know this, because I could feel the slapping of my hands against my sides, protecting my heart, pelvis and mouth. After an unknown period of time, it became overwhelming, I fought my way back to consciousness and prayed fervently, to make it STOP. The continuum of time, I can't share with any precise calculation, but it would be eight to nine hours before fully awakening.

God answered my prayer, and I found myself in a field of faces, young, old and all ages in between. Faces with grimacing, sad, and mortifying expressions. All repeating the same phrase, "Stand up help us!"

I don't believe that I have ever prayed as I did during those hours, what seemed like an eternity in pain, came to an end with a reckoning of my soul to my Creator. The voice was audible, palatable and piercing. You are mine!

I struggled to push back and to regain consciousness repeatedly, but each time, it was as though what had a grip on my psyche was stronger, pulling me deeper and deeper, until it stopped.

The journey through deep seeded repressed memories was over, the faces of all those in pain and suffering, became a crowd of familiar and unfamiliar faces, who ceased. All that was now seen were colleagues, people from my past, people I had not yet met, standing together, holding arms, with a multitude of others behind, pushing forward against the darkness, and in the midst, Peace, Grace and a renewing Hope.

The morning sunlight beat on my cheek, familiar voices roamed in the space, it was daylight. It was over. Purging is a natural facet of this process, but in my case, there had been no physical purge. The Shamanic healers, who were reportedly alongside me, shared their wisdom of our collective unconscious experience. They provided cleaning brews to purify my body and shared their wisdom, handed down to them by their ancestral heritage. I learned more about myself and my state of being in those few days, than I had in years of reflection and prayer.

Answers are not provided when we ask for them, but rather when we are ready to receive them. This was the beginning of my awakening.

Don't live your life in the past, numb to a reality that can be filled with joy, love and faith, despite fear. The greatest gift, is rebirthed renewal, through it you will discover what you were created and ordained to do in your lifetime on this planet. I can assure you it has little to do with yourself.

Being fully alive, is knowing the truth.

The truth that you were created in the image of God. The truth that there is purpose for your life. The truth that even though it may not seem like it at all times, you are never alone. The truth that when hardships come, because they are promised, you will prevail and be refined further into the masterpiece you were created to become. The truth that there is no other creation on this planet, by your name. The truth that until you take responsibility for your choices and change in alignment to your calling, you will wonder aimlessly, unfulfilled, accumulating experiences, things and people, who will never fill the void in your existence.

How do we begin our awakening?

<u>3 – Step to Awakening</u>

Y – You begin to awaken by taking responsibility for your choices, change etc.

O – You begin to awaken, by following your ordained path

U – You begin to awaken, by living out your uniqueness

My awakening continues to evolve daily. There is no longer ambivalence or drifting through life. Every moment has meaning, richness in gratitude with purpose. Does this mean that my life is easy-breezy, that I get everything that my heart desires? Absolutely not. Does it make me immune somehow to hardship? Again, the answer is no. But, now awakened, I appreciate, am grateful for, and know that I'm equipped to handle everything, anything that comes my way in life in communion with my Creator.

About Dr. Jessica Vera

Dr. J., a writer, entrepreneur, philanthropist and an unwavering optimistic visionary, believes in YOU.

Her platform from trauma to servant-leader, resulted in creation of several successful international for-profit companies; and her nonprofit flagship, Elite Foundation (headquarters in Florida). Elite Foundation creates a safe-haven for all who have suffered trauma from vulnerability to human exploitation in all its ugly forms. Elite's mission is to educate, empower and to promote survivors to evolve into all they were divinely ordained to be and find their voice.

Through Elite's three silos of goods and services, Dr. J. has taken her love of the arts (psychology, visual, emotive and intuitive, as well as entrepreuenralism) and cinematography and the written word, to create education, production and publishing services, delivered through advocacy and mentoring in collaboration with a multitude of professionals and parallel organizations, who share the vision of the movement to eradicate human exploitation in our generation #ItEndsWithUs

Dr. J. and Elite Foundation currently locks-shields with Warriors, who share her belief that the greatest gift of success in life is reciprocity. To Dr. J. success is measured not by things one accumulates; but by the souls we have the privilege of positively impacting through our life on this earth. She is a fervent believer in the power of prayer, has an unwavering adoration for her Creator and the Love that she has been shown and has the privilege to share with others willing to receive it. Dr. J.'s personal vision is to empower souls to live out their full potential in life and business, through socially-conscious business practices that create not only personal financial freedom, but funds freedom for those in need.

Dr. J. participates in her community, has spoken internationally and on domestic platforms throughout her 30-year career, and most recently taught in Washington, D.C. in support of efforts in the battle against Human Sex Trafficking.

Dr. J. is a Transformational Practitioner, who through her mastery & licensure of informed modalities, post-doctorate study of ancient practices and her proprietary Transformational Principle™ empiracally-based modality specifically for those desireous of eradicating the effects of trauma; she has helped thousands of souls, couples, families and corporations to transform and become more, by tapping into full potential.

Happily married for 20 years+, with two beautiful daughters, Dr. J. strives to intentionally live out a balance of love, life & passion-work.

To learn more about Dr. Jessica Vera please visit drjvera.com

To learn more about Elite Foundation please visit EliteFundsFreedom.org

Made in the
USA
Lexington, KY